Bamboo in Vietnam

This book presents interdisciplinary research on bamboo in Vietnam, drawing on the anthropology of gesture, ethnobotany and the history of technology.

The authors have adopted a technological approach which reviews how the terminology of different parts of the bamboo plant in the dictionaries in Romanized Vietnamese or in Vietnamese vernacular writing (nôm) enabled the authors to identify not only the plant but also each technical gesture for its appropriation by the artisan. Lithographic, literary and historical sources from the chronicles have been mobilized to illustrate the many uses of this versatile plant.

Richly illustrated throughout, this book will appeal to students and scholars of Vietnam, anthropology, the history of science and technology, environmental history and architecture. It will also be of great value to those interested in the applications of bamboo in the contemporary world.

Đinh Trọng Hiếu is an anthropologist and ethnobotanist. Until his retirement in 2003, he worked as a researcher at CNRS (National Center for Scientific Research).

Emmanuel Poisson is Professor of History at Paris Cité University, France, and Deputy Director at the French Research Institute on East Asia (IFRAE, UMR 8043).

Needham Research Institute Series

Series Editor: Christopher Cullen

Joseph Needham's 'Science and Civilisation' series began publication in the 1950s. At first it was seen as a piece of brilliant but isolated pioneering. However, at the beginning of the twenty-first century, it became clear that Needham's work had succeeded in creating a vibrant new intellectual field in the West. The books in this series cover topics that broadly relate to the practice of science, technology and medicine in East Asia, including China, Japan, Korea and Vietnam. The emphasis is on traditional forms of knowledge and practice, but without excluding modern studies that connect their topics with their historical and cultural context.

Speaking of Epidemics in Chinese Medicine
Disease and the geographic imagination in Late Imperial China
Marta E. Hanson

Reviving Ancient Chinese Mathematics
Mathematics, history and politics in the work of Wu Wen-Tsun
Jiri Hudecek

Rice, Agriculture and The Food Supply in Premodern Japan
The Place of Rice
Charlotte von Verschuer
Translated and edited by Wendy Cobcroft

The Politics of Chinese Medicine under Mongol Rule
Reiko Shinno

Asian Medical Industries
Contemporary Perspectives on Traditional Pharmaceuticals
Edited by Stephan Kloos and Calum Blaikie

The Chinese Astronomical Bureau, 1620–1850
Lineages, Bureaucracy and Technical Expertise
Ping-Ying Chang

www.routledge.com/Needham-Research-Institute-Series/book-series/SE0483

Bamboo in Vietnam

An Anthropological and Historical Approach

Đinh Trọng Hiếu and Emmanuel Poisson

Translated from French by Clare Perkins Cléret

LONDON AND NEW YORK

First published 2024
by Routledge
4 Park Square, Milton Park, Abingdon, Oxon OX14 4RN

and by Routledge
605 Third Avenue, New York, NY 10158

Routledge is an imprint of the Taylor & Francis Group, an informa business

© 2024 Đinh Trọng Hiếu and Emmanuel Poisson

The right of Đinh Trọng Hiếu and Emmanuel Poisson to be identified as
authors of this work has been asserted in accordance with sections 77 and
78 of the Copyright, Designs and Patents Act 1988.

All rights reserved. No part of this book may be reprinted or reproduced or
utilised in any form or by any electronic, mechanical, or other means, now
known or hereafter invented, including photocopying and recording, or in
any information storage or retrieval system, without permission in writing
from the publishers.

Trademark notice: Product or corporate names may be trademarks or
registered trademarks, and are used only for identification and explanation
without intent to infringe.

British Library Cataloguing-in-Publication Data
A catalogue record for this book is available from the British Library

ISBN: 978-1-032-39571-5 (hbk)
ISBN: 978-1-032-39572-2 (pbk)
ISBN: 978-1-003-35034-7 (ebk)

DOI: 10.4324/9781003350347

Typeset in Times New Roman
by Apex CoVantage, LLC

Contents

Table of illustrations	*vii*
Conventions	*xii*
List of abbreviations	*xiii*
Introduction: bamboo – tree or grass?	1

PART 1
Bamboo: an anthropological and historical approach   3

1	Bamboo, man, landscape	5
2	Terminology and technology: identification, uses, names – from naming to datation	17
3	Uses of bamboo according to its qualities	34
4	Bamboo as symbol	59
5	Bamboo and power	67

PART 2
Bamboo iconography   81

6	Bamboo used as it is, after felling	83
7	Uses of bamboo tube	108
8	Use of split bamboo cut into lengths	133
9	Basket-making	154
10	The Gia Định Art School contribution	197

vi *Contents*

PART 3
Contemporary bamboo 211

11 Bamboo at present 213

Conclusion: what status for bamboo? 220

Annexes *222*
Bibliography *230*
Index *236*

Illustrations

1.1	Wild bamboo at the foot of a limestone massif	6
1.2	Buffalo and clumps of bamboo on a dyke	6
1.3	Cross-section of a dwelling on a hillside	7
1.4–5	Knotty trunk with "three stars"	8–9
1.6–7	Trunks irregularly knotty at the base	10–11
1.8	The venerable Bùi Văn Cát, aged 82 in 1982, with his staff of old age	12
1.9	Clumps of bamboo at Gióng temple	14
1.10	Bas-relief sculpture in stone: clump of bamboo, pine tree	15
2.1	"nôm", summary table	18
2.2–3	A page from Alexandre de Rhodes' *Dictionarium* (1651), at the letter T and at the entry "tle"	20–21
2.4	Naming bamboo	24
2.5	Structure of bamboo and related technology	25
2.6–7	Postures while at work: a craftsman making bamboo frame lanterns	27–28
2.8	Craftsmen preparing strips of bamboo	28
2.9–10	Ethnic minority basket hod, Central Việt Nam	29–30
2.11–12	Two models of teapot baskets	30–31
2.13–14	Use of poor-quality inner strips for decoration	32
3.1	Bamboo hedge surrounding a dwelling, seen from inside	35
3.2	Double bamboo hedge, Đào Xá Village	36
3.3	Planting young bamboo on a bank	37
3.4	Simple raft made from bamboo trunks tied together	38
3.5	Bamboo rafts used by French military engineers as a pontoon bridge to cross the Black River, 1884	39
3.6–7	Lengths of bamboo for carrying water	40–41
3.8–9	Large waterwheels in the Northern Highlands and in Quảng Ngãi	42–43
3.10–11	Bamboo roof structure in Thanh Hà Village	43–44
3.12	Bamboo used for mounting a swing (Hà Nội, Quán Thánh temple)	44
3.13	Bamboo used for scaffolding at Cổ Loa (Hà Nội Province)	45

viii   *Illustrations*

3.14	Staff of Old Age made from "chicken leg" bamboo with the "three stars" at each internode	48
3.15	Knife handle made from full straight bamboo with the "three stars" at each internode	49
3.16	Why bamboo is sharp	50
3.17	A bamboo dry fence protecting against incursion from a tiger	51
3.18	Percussion instruments "đing pâng" made of bamboo tubes	53
3.19	The "pah pung" (or "klong put")	54
3.20	Suspended sound tubes struck by hammers activated by a waterfall	55
3.21–22	Uses of crushed bamboo: a hammock and a fence	56
3.23	Snare trap to catch birds	57
4.1	Flowering of a clump of bamboo, which then dies immediately	62
5.1–2	Palanquin made of bamboo strips	70
5.3	A rider carrying the Imperial post	73
6.1	Cutting bamboo shoots	84
6.2	Using a spade to dig up bamboo rhizomes	85
6.3	Cutting bamboo with a large knife	86
6.4	Land surveying	87
6.5	Village elder	88
6.6	Generation gap	89
6.7	Gathering leaves	90
6.8	Bamboo pole for lunar New Year	90
6.9	Displaying a head on a bamboo mast after beheading	91
6.10	Dismantling a bamboo raft	91
6.11	Transporting bundles of large bamboo	92
6.12	Shouldering bamboo trunks	92
6.13	Punting a bamboo raft	93
6.14–16	Bamboo swings	94–96
6.17	Watchtower	97
6.18	Rain gutter	98
6.19	Gutter or conduit	99
6.20	Why bamboo is sharp	99
6.21	Making a new roof	100
6.22	Bamboo ladder seller	101
6.23	Bridge for continuing on the way	102
6.24	Woman doing her washing from a bamboo pontoon	103
6.25	Bamboo weaponry	104
6.26	Bending a length of bamboo	105
6.27	Lifting a shrimping net (using a hooked stick)	106
7.1	Threshing soya beans with a bamboo flail	109
7.2	Child wearing a bamboo float to avoid drowning	110
7.3	A prisoner (carrying a cangue)	110

7.4	(Man) smoking a water pipe	111
7.5	Decorated water pipe	112
7.6	Pipe (in the shape of a) "tube", made from an old bamboo trunk	113
7.7	Drilling the stem of a pipe made of old dwarf bamboo	114
7.8	Piercing the diaphragm of a bamboo by hand to make a pipe stem	115
7.9	Hollowing a bamboo tube to make a blowpipe	116
7.10	Dog merchant	117
7.11	Putting a dog on a leash	118
7.12	The dog market	119
7.13	Perforating a bamboo trunk to make a tube	120
7.14	A cup in the shape of bamboo	121
7.15	Imitation bamboo earthenware teapot	121
7.16	Child firing a bamboo gun	122
7.17	Burning pieces of bamboo to prepare a decoction	123
7.18	Blowing into a duck's throat to facilitate plucking	124
7.19–22	Blowing into a tube to make sweetmeats and children's toys	125–127
7.23	Playing a flute/flute	127
7.24	Musician playing a side-blown flute	128
7.25	Bamboo used as notice board	129
7.26	Sealing a jar for soya sauce	130
7.27	Cauldron for rinsing water	131
8.1	Building a fence	134
8.2	Bamboo shade for siesta	135
8.3	Bamboo screen for veranda	136
8.4	Bamboo frame for constructing a plinth base	137
8.5	Enclosure for raising ducks	137
8.6	Fumigation using a decoction of leaves	138
8.7	Keeping a pig still to cut its throat	139
8.8	Bamboo torch used during sacrifices	140
8.9–10	Bamboo strip spills	141–142
8.11	Burning a ring around the neck to torture a prisoner	143
8.12	Maker of *ex-votos*	144
8.13	Musician setting the rhythm for a dance with two bamboo sticks	144
8.14	Professional percussionist playing the beat	145
8.15	Advertising wares in the street	145
8.16	Bamboo clips for grilling pork	146
8.17	Prawns on a skewer	147
8.18	Putting little freshwater crabs on pins	148
8.19	Splitting bamboo to make a fine-tooth comb	149
8.20	A comb (untitled)	150
8.21	Bamboo accessory for picking fruit	150

x *Illustrations*

8.22	Picking carambola	151
8.23	Bamboo frame paper lampshade	152
8.24	Bamboo tool for peeling cucurbits	153
9.1	Weaving an open-work basket	155
9.2	Bamboo drying rack for paper	156
9.3	Two craftsmen working bamboo	157
9.4	Weaving a bamboo fan	157
9.5	Making paper fans	158
9.6	Weaving the hull of a boat	161
9.7	Weaving a chicken coop	162
9.8	Weaving a partition or rack	162
9.9	Weaving a tray-cover with wire	163
9.10	Collecting water cabbage	164
9.11	Watering cabbages (using a basket to sprinkle the water)	165
9.12	Boat for crossing a river	166
9.13	Collecting lotus flowers (in a woven bamboo boat)	167
9.14	Carrying a basket boat (over the head)	168
9.15	Boating using short, curved oars	169
9.16	Bamboo basket-work oar	170
9.17	Pressing cooked rice in a flexible bamboo flake	170
9.18	Woven bamboo rack or trellis	171
9.19	Bamboo trellis fan	172
9.20	Round bamboo flake to hold paddy rice	172
9.21	Tipping paddy rice into a rolled flake cylinder	173
9.22	Restraining a dog for castration	174
9.23	Crate made of twisted bamboo	175
9.24	Closely woven bamboo basket for washing rice	175
9.25	Open weave bamboo basket for washing vegetables	176
9.26	Winnowing [rice chaff] or hollow paddy rice	177
9.27	Medium-sized, wide, flat bamboo basket ("cái nia")	178
9.28–29	Large, wide, flat bamboo basket ("cái nong") and its Chinese equivalent	178–179
9.30	Two people carrying a large, flat basket for paddy rice	179
9.31	Riddling rice	180
9.32–33	Riddle for drying goods and its Chinese equivalent	181
9.34	Sieving bran	182
9.35	Riddling coal to make fuel for the forge	183
9.36	Sieving granulated sugar	184
9.37–39	Mill for hulling rice and its operator	185–186
9.40	Bamboo cages for carrying pigs	186
9.41	Bamboo racks for drying rice paper	187
9.42	Frogs carried to market in a bamboo basket	188
9.43	Draining a fish pond, collecting snails	189
9.44–45	Fish trap with shafts	190–191
9.46	Fish Carafe-shaped trap	191

9.47	Trap for catching shrimps and fish	192
9.48–49	Bailer with rope handles for use by two people	192–193
9.50–52	Use of tripod bailer or water shovel	194–195
10.1	Vegetable cultivation at Bình Tây	198
10.2	Loading paddy rice into sacks	199
10.3	Monkey bridge over an arroyo at Sa Đéc	200
10.4	Large, square dipping net	201
10.5	Threshing rice	202
10.6	Hulling rice	203
10.7	Making bamboo rice grinders	204
10.8	Winnowing rice	205
10.9	Poultry seller	206
10.10	Peasant woman carrying her child in a basket	207
10.11	Corner kitchen with utensil holders in bamboo	208
10.12	Bamboo cupping equipment	209
11.1	Display of bamboo household goods	214
11.2	Fish traps	214
11.3	Bamboo screens in an ethnic minority Kà-tu home	215
11.4–6	Three bamboo buildings designed by the architect Võ Trọng Nghĩa	216–217
11.7	Kaly Tran and lithophone with bamboo sound box	218
11.8	Kaly Tran playing the bamboo xylophone ("đàn t'rưng")	219
12.1	Grinder, its parts and their names	223
12.2	Making fire by rubbing a sliver of bamboo on wood	224
12.3	Knife for buffalo sacrifice	225
12.4	Buffalo bell	225
12.5	Hen coop	226
12.6	Basket market. Northern Việt Nam	226
12.7	New, roughly cut carrying poles	227
12.8	New, carafe-shaped traps, sold at market. Vinh market	227
12.9	Carafe-shaped trap (Phú Thọ Province)	228
12.10	Hook made in one piece from base of bamboo trunk	228

Conventions

- Double quotation marks are used at the beginning and end of a quoted passage.
- Words in the vernacular in Vietnamese, Chinese, Japanese, Khmer (or the ethnic minorities of these countries) are enclosed in double quotation marks ". . .". For example, "mei zhu (mai trúc)", "shakuhachi", "treay", "t'rưng". Certain words in a scientific context are also enclosed in double quotation marks such as "straw", "grass" or "trunk".
- Italics are reserved for the titles of publications or for the two-word scientific names of plants (in Latin). Other particular conventions are mentioned at the beginning of the paragraphs in question, as well as the typography; notably, in Part Two.
- Names: for Chinese authors or authors from Chinese regions, the "pinyin" transcription is used; for example: Liang Shaoren. The names of the regions mentioned in the texts (translated from Chinese) are written in "pinyin" alongside the Sino-Vietnamese terms; for example: Jiuren (Cửu Chân), without quotation marks. Spelling for names in Vietnamese will be according to accepted usage: Lê Quý Đôn, Lê Hữu Trác, but Tự Đức, Hùng Vương (and not Hùng-vương). For the names of ethnic groups in Vietnam, a Western spelling has been avoided, retaining: Rhade (and not Rades), Mường (and not Muong). However, for the title of the book, the spelling for Vietnam has been slightly modified for editorial reasons.

Abbreviations

ANOM	Archives Nationales d'Outre-Mer (Aix-en-Provence)
BV	*Bạch vân am quốc ngữ thi tập*
cb	*chính biên*
ĐKĐDC	*Đông Khánh địa dư chí*
Đ.T.H.	Đinh Trọng Hiếu
Figure	Figure
f °	folio
Gouv. Gén.	Gouverneur Général
ms.	manuscript
T.N.	translator's note
Phot.	Photograph
PBTL	*Phủ biên tạp lục*
pl.	plate
q.	*quyển (book)*
sv.	sino-vietnamese
tb	*tiền biên*
TL	*Đại Nam thực lục*
TT	*Đại Việt sử ký toàn thư*
VĐLN	*Vân Đài loại ngữ*
vn.	vietnamese
vol.	volume

Introduction

Bamboo – tree or grass?

As the wide variety of themes explored in this book may be confusing for the reader, we would like to use these few lines to explain our interdisciplinary approach. Every culture – and no-one needs to be reminded of this – uses specific terms for all the plants present in its environment. The bamboo growing in Việt Nam is not a plant that stands out from the vegetation surrounding it; on the contrary, it blends in with the landscape. Two vernacular expressions are used to designate all plants: "cây cỏ" (cây = tree, cỏ = grass) or "cây cối" (cây = tree, cối = grass, taken from Chinese). For the same designation, Chinese uses the binome "cao mu" (cao 艸 = grass, mu 木 = tree, wood). Although botanists classify bamboo with grasses, most people in Việt Nam automatically associate bamboo "tre" with the classifier "cây" (tree); bamboo is therefore considered to be a tree "cây tre",[1] even though other plants up to two metres in height are described as grasses: "cỏ tranh" (*Imperata cylindrica*), for example.

So, height is not in itself sufficient as a characteristic to describe a tree. Grasses are pliable, but not bamboo, which returns to its original straight position; it's a "tree" but a flexible, elastic[2] tree, whereas true wood is rigid and stable. Bamboo cannot be substituted for the reed in the oak/reed pair because the reed, which is also a grass, is weak, whereas bamboo has a strong trunk and can withstand a gale. Other characteristics of the structure of this trunk distinguish bamboo from a tree: a tree is woody, growing from the inside of the trunk towards the softer outside, whereas bamboo, like all grasses, develops from the outside inwards, where there is less resistance. The observation is fundamental because all technical know-how depends on this. To fell a woody plant or a bamboo man uses an intermediary tool in stone or metal (stone axe, hatchet, knife, saw), the aim being to separate the trunk from its base. The difference with bamboo resides in its longitudinal fibres: when struck with an axe or a knife, its trunk splits easily lengthwise, in spite of the many knots, while lengthwise sawing of a tree trunk requires considerable effort.

Another rule can be observed in all societies in contact with vegetation: the more a plant – preferably a useful one, but not necessarily – is familiar, the more details are observed and the more names these details are given, as is the case with bamboo and with rice. The widest possible review of terminology can enable not only identification of the plant but also each technical action involved in the appropriation of the plant in question. This research is possible, thanks to the existence of

DOI: 10.4324/9781003350347-1

2 Introduction

old lexographies in Romanized Vietnamese ("quốc ngữ") or in vernacular writing ("nôm"). This indigenous classification has been used as the basis of the chapters in Part 1 of the book concentrating on the historical and anthropological approach to bamboo. In Part 2, instead of describing technical action in detail, iconography takes precedence. The wood engravings of artisans in the north of Việt Nam in Henri Oger's compilation (*Technique du peuple annamite*, 1909) and the lithographs in *Monographie dessinée de l'Indochine* (1935) were chosen to illustrate the multiple uses of the plant. In both sections of the book, we have started from the plant as a whole to conclude with bamboo as felled, sawn, split and woven into basketware. The organization of the contents of the book is based on technology. The cross-referencing of texts and fieldwork observation is inspired by the procedure followed by scholars in the classical period in Việt Nam; namely, Tuệ Tĩnh (1330–1400) and Lê Quý Đôn (1726–1784).

Thus, in the study of the latter, a learned encyclopaedist, the uses of bamboo tinder ("cây đóm") as a starting point in his *Categorized Sayings from the library* [Vân đài loại ngữ 蕓臺類語] in the 18th century, is typical of this method. Poems, historical works of the Lê and Nguyễn periods, monographies, atlas, flora, text books from 4th to the 19th century demonstrate the diversity of uses of the plant.

Nevertheless, our work does not claim to be exhaustive: new uses may come to light, and we may have made our own omissions. Another obstacle to our investigations: the establishment of texts and textual criticism is sadly lacking concerning the study of Vietnamese language and culture, both ancient and modern. We hope this book, a result of the collaboration between an ethnobotanist and a historian, will arouse the curiosity of the reader and inspire new fields of research.

Notes

1 As in China from the Tang dynasty onwards (Su Jing, pp. 103–4). Before this, uncertainty reigns: in some ancient texts, such as the *Shanhaijing* 山海經 (Yuan Ke, p. 26), it is considered to be a grass (cao 草), then later, as a plant in its own category. Dai Kaizhi 戴凱之 of the Western Jin (265–317), author of a *Treatise on Bamboo* [Zhupu 竹譜], says that is "neither grass nor tree" 非草非木, and his contemporary, Ji Han 稽含, a minister under Emperor Hui of the Jin dynasty (290–306), author of the *Nanfang Caomu Zhuang* 南方草木狀, has a separate group for bamboo.
2 Much more so than a banana plant.

Part 1

Bamboo: an anthropological and historical approach

1 Bamboo, man, landscape

There are few plants that fit so perfectly into the landscape in Việt Nam as bamboo, whether in the plains or in the mountains. Bamboo groves display a mass of delicate, pale-green foliage that stands out from other plants, their treetops fluttering even in the gentlest breeze. Whether wild or cultivated, plant and man seem to be in balance: as it grows, it provides a natural background for habitation, and when felled for use as a building material for enclosures or houses, it attenuates man's harsh domination of the natural environment, differing in this respect from wood, brick, cement or concrete. This harmony is the result of long coexistence. The geographer Pierre Gourou, writing eloquently on this interaction, observed both in the north and in the south of the country:

> The village is surrounded by a bamboo hedge whose close spiny stalks provide an efficient barrier against thieves. The villagers tend the hedge carefully and heavy fines are imposed on any unauthorized person who dares to cut down a bamboo. [. . .] At the same time as it protects the villagers from outside danger, the hedge represents a sort of sacred perimeter for the village community, a sign of its individuality and its independence. If a village has participated in agitation in times of unrest or given asylum to rebels the prime punishment inflicted is the obligation to cut down the bamboo hedge. This constitutes a serious blow to self-respect, and is considered shameful; the village community is in as embarrassing a situation as a human being stripped of his clothing and abandoned naked in a fully dressed crowd.[1]

During the agricultural reforms in the north of Việt Nam between 1953 and 1980, villagers removed these traditional hedges and were encouraged by ingenious agronomists to replace them with filao. However, this policy was unsuccessful, not only because filaos have no uses, whereas bamboo groves have many, but also because filaos require an enormous amount of water and are an insult to the landscape. Nowadays, bamboo is no longer used for protective hedges around villages, but it is still planted in gardens, and the right variety is chosen according to needs. One can often observe, for example, that, for the same hedge, in the case of a dwelling situated on a hillside (see Figure 1.3), the bamboo planted higher up and behind the house is shorter (7 metres, maximum), branches are lopped to thicken

DOI: 10.4324/9781003350347-3

6 *Bamboo: an anthropological and historical approach*

Figure 1.1 Wild bamboo at the foot of a limestone massif. Chùa Thầy. Hà Tây Province. 1979. Photograph by Đinh Trọng Hiếu.

Figure 1.2 Buffalo and clumps of bamboo on a dyke. Đồng Xâm village. Thái Bình Province. 1979. Photograph by Đinh Trọng Hiếu.

Bamboo, man, landscape 7

Figure 1.3 Cross-section of a dwelling on a hillside. 1: *Bambusa multiplex* ("hóp"), 25: *Bambusa stenostachya* ("tre gai, tre nhà"). 1982. Drawing by Đinh Trọng Hiếu.

the growth and, in this case, *Bambusa multiplex* ("hóp")[2] is used. For the front of the dwelling lower down, a different bamboo with long stalks is used, and its foliage protects the house from the rays of the setting sun when this is required by the topography of the location; in this case, *Bambusa stenostachya* ("tre gai, tre nhà") is used, as it can grow up to 20m in height.

As regards the production of "bamboo shoots", or spears, such as *Gigantochloa levis* ("bương") or the enormous *Dendrocalamus giganteus Munro* ("mai"), a spacious garden is necessary. Preferable to these is bamboo of more modest dimensions whose trunks have various technical uses, such as *Bambusa variabilis* ("tầm vông"); it can be a food crop, a technical material and a decorative element. As well as the shoots being edible, this bamboo has good internode sections for use as poles, pipe stems, rods or slats. So, from north to south, the right bamboo for the job at hand can always be found, not only because it is available for sale but also frequently, particularly in the countryside, it can probably be found in one's own garden. People with a bamboo grove at home have a multi-purpose toolbox available as well as a healthy "savings account": as soon as some cash is needed, a few bamboos can be sold, and what is more, these "savings" regenerate independently. A bamboo grove, once it is established, demands the minimum of attention and provides a maximum return on investment!

For the peasant farmer, bamboo is readily available as a cheap, multi-purpose building material. Although the trunk of *Melia azedarach* takes ten years to mature into excellent wood for construction and is therefore more expensive, it is possible to grow the quantity of bamboo required for a house of similar size, including fence, stakes for the garden and domestic implements, in a third of the time (and it costs far less). However, the reasons for the presence of small clumps of various different types of bamboo in a kitchen garden are not always simply utilitarian. Ordinary people grow *Bambusa ventricosa* ("trúc đùi gà", see Figures 1.4 and 1.6)

8   *Bamboo: an anthropological and historical approach*

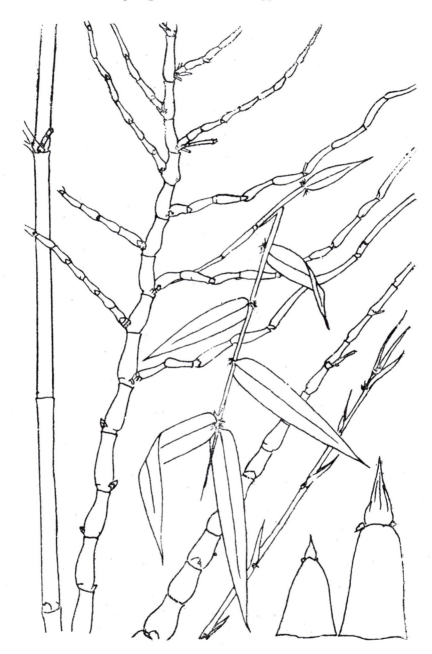

Figures 1.4–5 Knotty trunk with "three stars (tam tinh 三星)" (on the left). Lê Khả Kế et al., 1975, pp. 184, 271. The botanical drawings (on the left) are taken from the referenced work (Lê Khả Kế et al., 1975, pp. 184, 271); the drawing on the right is by Đinh Trọng Hiếu.

Bamboo, man, landscape 9

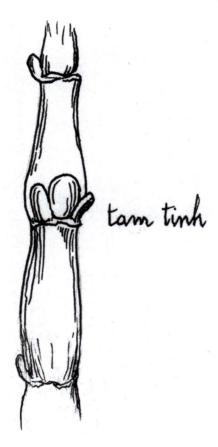

Figures 1.4–5 (Continued)

or *Phyllostachis bambusoïdes* ("trúc hóa long", see Figure 1.5) in this way for aesthetic reasons. Among the knotty trunks of the former, a regular stalk with regular swellings at each knot is carefully chosen, where developing side shoots show the particular "three stars (tam tinh)" formation to be used as a "staff of old age" – the walking stick an elderly person can lean on to get about; its regularity is a source of pride, and it will last beyond the end of their earthly existence. Rolf Stein states that "the Taoist has his double: his staff. [. . .] Bamboo is also a symbol of longevity and a talisman against evil".[3]

The second bamboo provides trunks that are strangely knotty at the base. They are highly prized to make walking sticks, coat stands and curios.

Learning about the different varieties of bamboo adapted for each use and the preferred choice of mutant varieties, often with polymorphous trunks, has been the result of a long process, from an early appropriation of the plant, certainly since prehistoric times, or at least since before historical time. Fragments of pottery bearing

10 *Bamboo: an anthropological and historical approach*

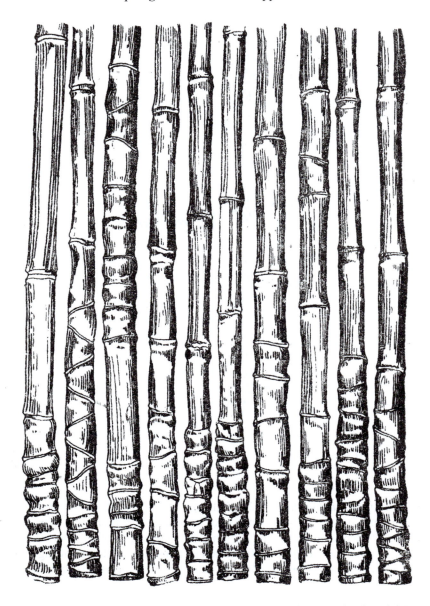

Figure 1.6–7 Trunks irregularly knotty at the base (on the right). Drawing by Đinh Trọng Hiếu. The botanical drawings (on the left) are taken from the referenced work (Lê Khả Kế et al., 1975, p. 271); the drawing on the right is by Đinh Trọng Hiếu.

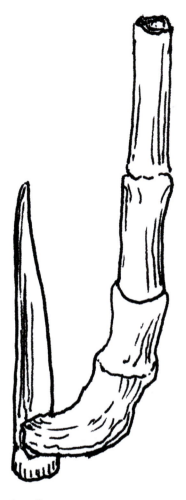

Figures 1.6–7 (Continued)

the imprint of basketwork similar to the modern basketwork made with bamboo strips have been unearthed at sites at Đa Bút and Lũng Hòa. These fragments could have been used as a basis for study if only they had been dated correctly; this is all the more unfortunate in that they exist in several stages of elaboration: terracotta fragments, fired at a low heat, bearing traces of basket-ware; pieces from vessels bearing traces of basket-ware on the base; potsherds with basket-ware decoration.

12 *Bamboo: an anthropological and historical approach*

Figure 1.8 The venerable Bùi Văn Cát, aged 82 in 1982, with his staff of old age. Đào Xá. Phú Thọ Province. Photograph by Đinh Trọng Hiếu.

However, a question remains unanswered: was the use of bamboo possible without the use of metal implements, and if so, then in what way?

Indeed, as we shall see later, an examination of the structure of bamboo leads to two observations: one can neither break nor work bamboo with bare hands. In order to craft it, a person needs a harder tool than his or her hand to first fell and then cut it. From early times and still now, bamboo is worked using a blade; and with such ease that one has to ask whether this would have been possible before the existence of knives and metal. A few minor operations, such as breaking off strips, can be achieved with the teeth, but it would be foolhardy to attempt to use one's teeth to fell or split a trunk. The existence of shaped pebbles and the shards of these same stones in many sites dating from the Hoabinhian[4] period may indicate that these stones were used to fell and cut up bamboo. In that case, it could have been worked after felling, splitting and cutting the bamboo into rods or strips. Using these same pebbles (and/or pebble shards) once they have been split, then shaped and polished, it has been possible to experiment with making holes in a bamboo trunk and even assembling several lengths. Bamboo divided into strips or rods provides the material for basket-ware or for making other tools: knives, arrows, spears or poles. Finding this "missing link" in the development of the use of bamboo is the result of multi-disciplinary research in partnership with the research team at the Archaeological Institute of Việt Nam.[5] So the use of stone tools enabled various populations in south-east Asia to master the plant before the appropriation of metal and its use for tools.

The "Legend of Thánh Gióng", a story familiar to the Vietnamese and to researchers on Việt Nam, illustrates this point clearly and is worth a closer look. Gióng, a mythical hero in the no-less-mythical times of the Hùng kings, was born of an unknown father, and at the age of three, could neither walk nor speak. But one day, all of a sudden, on hearing the sovereign's herald proclaim that the kingdom was threatened and in need of someone to save it from invasion, Gióng started to speak to his mother, telling her to ask the king to provide a horse, a sword, an armour and a helmet, all made of the same iron. To everyone's surprise, the king agreed, and little Gióng immediately demanded dish upon dish of rice. As he ate, he grew and grew and became a giant. From then on, the only garment that would fit him was the armour. He jumped on the horse, put on his helmet and massacred many enemies while his horse blew fire from its nostrils, burning down several neighbouring forests. When his iron sword broke, Gióng pulled up clumps of bamboo and used them to stun the invaders. He then rose into heaven carried by his steed. Place names and flora attest to this: close to the battlefield, we find "Burned Village (Làng Cháy)", and there are still several clumps of bamboo within the boundaries of the holy site at Phù Đổng, where commemorative jousts are held every year in honour of Gióng. Popular opinion maintains that flames bursting from the nostrils of Gióng's horse transformed the green of the bark into the colour of scorched bamboo. Everyone is free to go and visit the vast temple near Hà Nội devoted to Gióng and to take photos of the ever-present bamboo!

The legend of Gióng is emblematic of the place given to these two materials: iron and bamboo. The iron horse has only one quality in battle: its nostrils blow fire, fire that is linked to the mastery of the forge. When its flies up to heaven, it becomes a bird or a kite and no longer has the intrinsic qualities of the horse, and it loses the weighty quality of metal. The iron helmet had no useful role and the iron sword broke at the height of the battle to be replaced appropriately by an uprooted

14 *Bamboo: an anthropological and historical approach*

Figure 1.9 Clumps of bamboo ("tre là ngà") at Gióng temple. Phù Đổng Village, Gia Lâm District, Hà Nội Province. 1989. Photograph by Đinh Trọng Hiếu.

clump of bamboo used as a club. These details are by no means fortuitous: Gióng, despite his Herculean strength, did not break the bamboo. He tore it out of the ground and used it as it was. In demonstrations of strength in various "martial arts" where the star event entails breaking piles of bricks, tiles, planks of wood or blocks of concrete, trunks of bamboo have never been used. There is a solid reason behind this, linked to the quality of bamboo that "bends but does not break".

Bamboo, as an easily sourced material, was also companion to the ingenious workmanship of local craftsmen. Early written sources up to the 20th century show the wide range of uses of the bi-products of the plant in public and private spheres since earliest times: crafts, arms and infrastructure. But its use always runs parallel with a certain spirit of wisdom: the plant does not dominate, neither visually nor spatially, being of modest proportions, nor is its deportment aggressive. The several qualities of bamboo, being both straight and supple but also tenacious, not only symbolize the countryside and virtues required of the scholar but also harmony with the environment. A passage from *Complete Book of the Historical Records of Đại Việt* concerning the frequent use of bamboo as an ornamental plant in conjunction with the pine tree is reminiscent of the "Garden of Curiosities" in the Europe of the Enlightenment. In the Quý Mão Year (1363), sixth [of the Đại Trị era] in the reign of Dụ Tông of the Trần, at the tenth moon, the emperor gave orders and

> a lake was excavated in the Imperial park near the women's quarter. In this stretch of water, rocks were installed to simulate a mountain with openings

Figure 1.10 Bas-relief sculpture in stone: from left to right, clump of bamboo, pine tree. Bút Tháp Pagoda. Bắc Ninh. 1982. Photograph by Đinh Trọng Hiếu.

on all four sides so that water could circulate freely. On the banks, pines, bamboo, all sorts of trees and unusual flowers were planted. A host of rare birds and strange animals were raised there. To the west of the lake, two cinnamon trees were planted and, in front of the Palace, a double cinnamon tree. This place bore the name of Palace of Tranquillity and Purity, and the lake was given the same name. Another smaller pond was dug and, with the assistance of locals from the East Lake district, it was filled with salt water for raising hawksbill sea turtles ("đồi mồi" 玳瑁), fish, soft-shelled trionyx ("biết" 鱉), sea crabs and other sea creatures. Inhabitants from Hóa Châu were also brought in and they acclimatized crocodiles. A lake called Pure Fishes was created for raising crucian carp ("phụ" 鮒).[6] A director responsible for the whole site was appointed, the post being created particularly to this end.[7]

It is not surprising that Nguyễn Trãi, one of the most celebrated scholars – also a statesman, a philosopher and a poet – spoke quite simply about the presence of bamboo in his life. He served as a high-ranking mandarin at the court of the Later Lê in the 15th century and, after taking part in the liberation of the country from the Ming invaders, he retired to the Côn Sơn mountains to live in harmony with nature. He wrote poetry there in the vernacular to celebrate a life respecting the ideals of wisdom: "By the open-work palisade (of my home), there are two clumps of dwarf bamboo; on my low bed, a pot of sweet herbs. Gibbons and birds keep me

16 *Bamboo: an anthropological and historical approach*

company in this solitary world. To the sound of my lute, books at my side, the days and months pass peacefully".[8]

籬疎疎𤾓欛竹 Giậu thưa thưa hai khóm trúc,
床塔塔蔑坆香 Giường thấp thấp một nồi hương.
猿鴀結伴嫩渃瓊 Vượn chim kết bạn non nước quạnh,
琴冊共饒時腦長 Cầm sách cùng nhau ngày tháng trường.

"Ordinary bamboo for poles, dwarf bamboo for the house. The days and months pass joyfully. Rice provided by inhuman hands: not to be eaten. Clothes obtained from faithless ones: above all not to be worn[9]".

筎濫棹竹濫茹 Vầu làm chèo, trúc làm nhà
特趣盃時腦戈 Được thú vui ngày tháng qua
飪几不仁咹倚渚 Cơm kẻ bất nhân, ăn ấy chớ
襖得無義默庄𨔋 Áo người vô nghĩa, mặc chẳng thà

Notes

1 Gourou, 1936, pp. 249–50.
2 For each variety of bamboo mentioned, as well as its common name, we give the botanical binomial, with or without the author's name. This can help the reader with research on internet or elsewhere to find out more.
3 Stein, 1987, pp. 103–4.
4 The Hoabinhian period has been dated between 8000–9000 years BCE, cf. Đinh, 1985, pp. 288–9.
5 See Đinh, 2009, pp. 24–31.
6 "Dai mei/đồi mồi" 玳瑁: the hawksbill sea turtle (*Eretmochelys imbricata*) is still known locally as Caret, Karet or Carette. 'Bie/biết' 鼈": Trionyx or Chinese softshell turtle: *Pelodiscus sinensis* (Wiegmann) or *Trionyx sinensis* (Wiegmann) or *Amyda sinensis* (Wiegmann). 鮒 is the abbreviation of "fu yu/phụ ngư" 鮒魚, the name of the goldfish: *Carassius auratus* (Linné).
7 *TT*, bản kỷ, q. VII, f ° 26a.
8 Nguyễn Trai, 1987, *Tức sự* (Present sentiments), 126. 1–4.
9 Nguyễn Trai, 1987, *Trần tình* (From the Heart), 39. 1–4.

2 Terminology and technology
Identification, uses, names – from naming to datation

Naming is an integral part of the process of identification when first coming into contact with a natural object, be it plant or animal. So, for bamboo, not only is the plant itself given a name but so are its different parts and the various operations performed in order to use it.

We can be sure that this knowledge goes back a long way because of the numerous names given to bamboo. However, in the case of Việt Nam, finding out about the names in early times is problematic because they are in vernacular, and at the time, there was no existent writing system for the common tongue. For centuries, the transmission of knowledge remained willingly oral or was carried out using the medium of Chinese characters. References to certain plants have been found in books written in Chinese, some using dimidiation; this is the case for the name of Canarium, "klam" (the early pronunciation in Vietnamese) dimidiated in two Chinese characters "橄欖 gan lan (sv. cảm lãm)". In order to transcribe their language, the Vietnamese developed their own writing system from a basis of sinograms. The earliest recognized document in vernacular writing ("nôm" 喃) dates from the early 11th century. However, according to more recent research, it first began to develop in the 9th and 10th centuries.[1] Let us quickly recall the mechanisms of how characters are formed. Some have been borrowed directly from Chinese; others have been created.

Characters borrowed from Chinese.

A1. Borrowed from Chinese in the "Hán-Việt" (Sino-Vietnamese) pronunciation and meaning as in the examples 才 ("tài") "talent" or 仁 ("nhân") meaning "humanity".[2]
A2. Borrowed from Chinese in the so-called "phi Hán-Việt"[3] pronunciation and meaning, as in the case of 房 (bedroom) whereas the "phi Hán-Việt" pronunciation was "buồng".[4]
A3. Transcription by homophone: the pronunciation of the character in "nôm" and the Sino-Vietnamese pronunciation coincide as in the example 些 ("ta") or 卒 ("tốt") but the meaning is different. 些 ("ta") in Sino-Vietnamese means "little" and in Vietnamese, "me". Similarly, ("tốt") in Sino-Vietnamese means "soldier"; in Vietnamese, "good".

DOI: 10.4324/9781003350347-4

18 Bamboo: an anthropological and historical approach

"nôm" characters										
borrowed from Chinese					creation of characters					
sound borrow				sound abandon	sound borrow		sound abandon	sound borrow		
A1	A2	A3	A4	A5	B1	B2	B3	B41	B42	B43
仁	房	些	芒	葉	朩	纇	睁	笝	糫	幣
nhân	buồng	ta	măng	lá	mọc	blái	nhòm	tre	bún	chợ
sound borrow		sound abandon		meaning borrow	meaning abandon		meaning borrow			
X	X	X	X	X	朩+<	巴+賴	目+穿	竹+知	米+罘	助+市

Figure 2.1 "nôm", summary table. Created by the author.

A4. Transcription by paraphone: the pronunciation of the "nôm" character and the Sino-Vietnamese pronunciation differ slightly as in the case of 級 and 南. In Sino-Vietnamese, 級 is pronounced "cấp" and means "degree". The same character in Vietnamese is pronounced "khớp" and means "bit, muzzle". Similarly, 南 in Sino-Vietnamese is pronounced "nam" and means "south". The same character in Vietnamese can be pronounced "nơm" and means "carafe-shaped trap". Similarly, 芒 in Sino-Vietnamese is pronounced "mang" and means "reed, blade, point". The same character in Vietnamese is pronounced "măng" and means "bamboo shoot".

A5. Simple characters were created by borrowing sinograms from Chinese and retaining the meaning but with a different pronunciation, as in the case of 葉 (plant leaf). Sino-Vietnamese pronunciation is "diệp" and the Vietnamese pronunction is "lá".

B. Created characters

B1. Characters with diacritical marks
These are improvements on the A4 group. The diacritical marks prevent confusion concerning the same character between the Sino-Vietnamese pronunciation and its distortion.
There are three of them[5]:
– The diacritical mark "cá" 个 as in the case of 黔 ("mỏ").[6]
– The diacritical mark "cá nháy" as in the case of 朩 ("mọc").

B2. Both elements are phonetic
In this case, two sinograms are associated each retaining the Sino-Vietnamese pronunciation. Three subcategories can be identified.
B2.1. Combination of two homophone or paraphone sinograms to create a "nôm" character. So 洔 ("gì") combines 之 ("chi") and 夷 ("di").

Terminology and technology 19

B2.2. Combination of two sinograms to create a "nôm" character follow-ing the "fan qie" (反切) procedure. In this case, the first character provides the initial consonant and the second character provides the rhyme: thus 膾 ("vùi") is the result of joining 尾 ("vĩ") and 會 ("hội").

B2.3. Other characters are created in the same way, but in this case, the first sinogram is used to express the initial element in the consonant group whereas the second is used to express the final element and the rhyme. Thus 麻 "**m**lời" (speech) is built with "ma" 麻 and "lợi" 利, 贔 "blái" (fruit) is built with "ba" 巴 and with "lại" 賴 and one of the early forms of "trái" which is found in the poems of Trần Nhân Tông (r.1278–1293).[7]

B3. Both elements are semantic
Thus 瞦 (to look) pronounced "nhòm" is composed of 目 (eye) and 穿 (to cross). In the same manner 仝 (clan chief) is pronounced "trùm" composed with two elements 人 (man) and 上 (above).

B4. Some characters are composed with a semantic and a phonetic element.

B4.1. Both elements are Chinese: a radical expressing the meaning and a character to express the sound.
Thus, 箉 (bamboo), which is pronounced "tre", is composed with a semantic element 竹, Chinese radical meaning "bamboo" and a pho-netic element 知 ("tri"). In the same manner, 鴲 (bird), pronounced "chim", is made up of a semantic element 鳥, a Chinese radical meaning "bird" and a phonetic element 占 ("chiêm"). In the same way 箝 (carafe-shaped trap), which is pronounced "nơm", is made with a semantic element 竹, a Chinese radical meaning "bamboo" and a phonetic element 南 ("nam"). In the same manner, 蕃 (cucur-bit, gourd), pronounced "dưa", is composed of a semantic element 艹, a Chinese radical meaning "plant", and a phonetic element 番 ("dư").

B4.2. The phonetic element is "nôm"; the semantic element is Chinese.
Thus, 唭 (speech), pronounced "lời", is made up of a semantic ele-ment, the radical 口 (mouth) and a phonetic element 圣 ("tlời, blời, trời-giời"). In the same way, 糧 (vermicelli), pronounced "bún", is made up of a semantic element, the radical 米 (rice) and a phonetic element 罞 ("bốn").

B4.3. In other cases, no sinogram in the "nôm" character is a radical. Thus, 幚 (market), pronounced "chợ", is composed of a semantic element 市 (market) and a phonetic element 助 ("trợ"). In the same way, 㕍 (three), pronounced "ba", is composed of a semantic element 三 (three) and a phonetic element 巴 ("ba").

So, "tre", one of the words for bamboo, has been written four different ways: 知, 箉, 椥, or 樓.[8]

From the 17th century onwards, along with "nôm" and classical Chinese, mis-sionaries from Europe, mainly from Spain, Portugal and France used the Latin

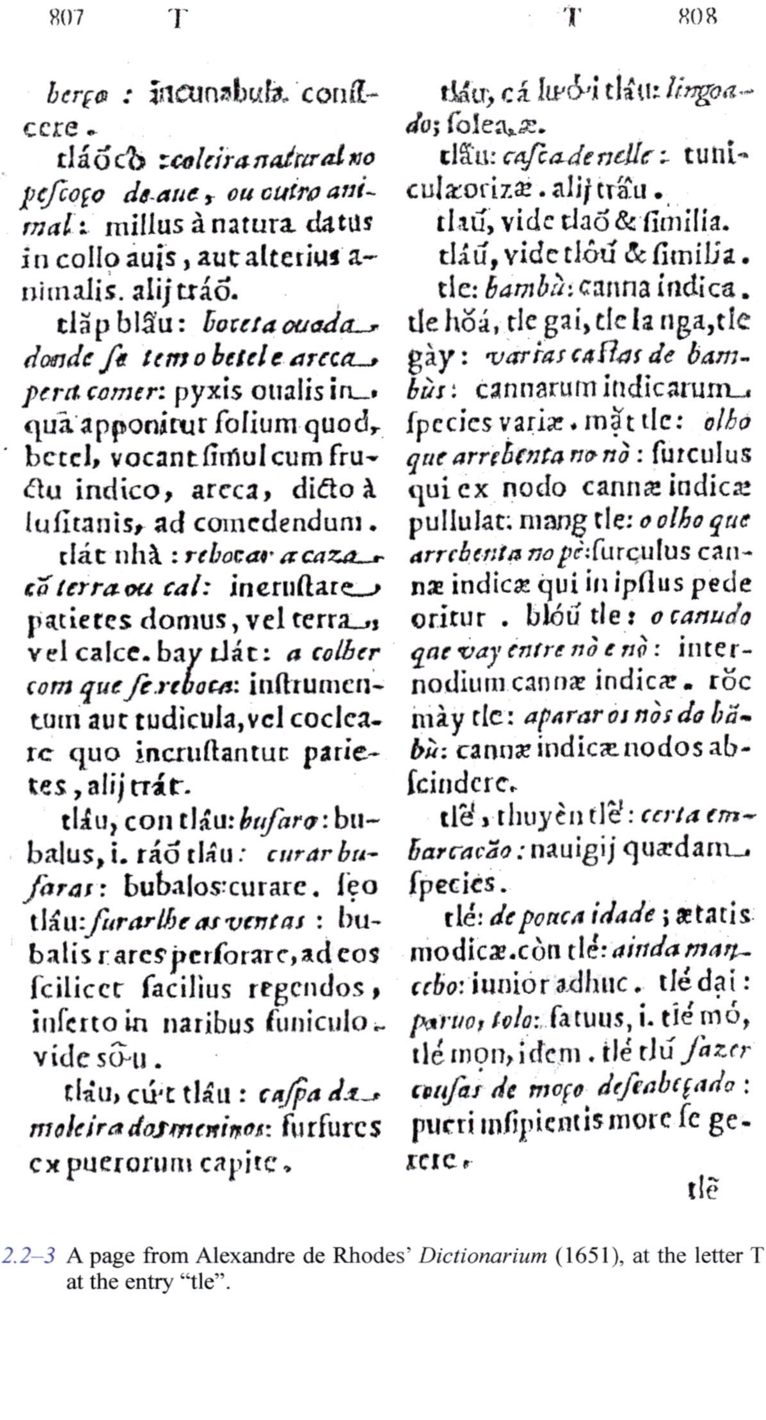

807 T   T 808

berço : incunabula. confi-
cere.

tláő cŏ :*coleira natural no
pefcoço de aue, ou outro animal*: nullus à natura datus
in collo auis, aut alterius a-
nimalis. alij tráő.

tlăp blău: *botesa ouada,
donde fe tem o betel e areca,
pera comer*: pyxis oualis in
quã apponitur folium quod,
betel, vocant fimul cum fru-
ctu indico, areca, dicto à
lufitanis, ad comedendum.

tlát nhà : *rebocar a caza,
cõ terra ou cal*: ineruftare
patietes domus, vel terra,
vel calce. bay tlát: *a colher
com que fe reboca*: inftrumen-
tum aut tudicula,vel coclea-
re quo incruftantur parie-
tes, alij trát.

tláu, con tláu: *bufaro*: bu-
balus, i. ráő tláu: *curar bu-
faras*: bubalos:curare. feo
tláu: *furarlhe as ventas* : bu-
balis rares perforare, ad eos
fcilicet facilius regendos,
inferto in naribus funiculo,
vide sŏu.

tláu, cút tláu : *cafpa da,
moleira dosmeninos*: furfures
ex puerorum capite.

tláu, cá ludi tláu: *lingoa-
do*; folea, æ.

tlău: *cafcadenelle*: tuni-
culæorizæ. alij tráu.

tláu, vide tlaő & fimilia.

tláu, vide tlóu & fimilia.

tle: *bambù*: canna indica.
tle hŏá, tle gai, tle la nga,tle
gày: *varias caftas de bam-
bùs*: cannarum indicarum,
fpecies variæ. mặt tle: *olho
que arrebenta no nò*: furculus
qui ex nodo cannæ indicæ
pullulat: mang tle: *o olho que
arrebenta no pè*:furculus cannæ indicæ qui in ipflus pede
oritur . blóu tle: *o canudo
que vay entre nò e nò*: inter-
nodium cannæ indicæ. rŏc
mày tle: *aparar os nòs do bã-
bù*: cannæ indicæ nodos ab-
fcindere.

tlě , thuyèn tlě: *certa em-
barcacão*: nauigij quædam,
fpecies.

tlé: *de ponca idade*; ætatis
modicæ.còn tlé: *ainda man-
cebo*: iunior adhuc. tlé dại:
paruo, tolo: fatuus, i. tlé mó,
tlé mon, idem. tlé tlú *fazer
coufas de moço defeabeçado*:
pueri infipientis more fe ge-
rcie.

tlě

Figure 2.2–3 A page from Alexandre de Rhodes' *Dictionarium* (1651), at the letter T and at the entry "tle".

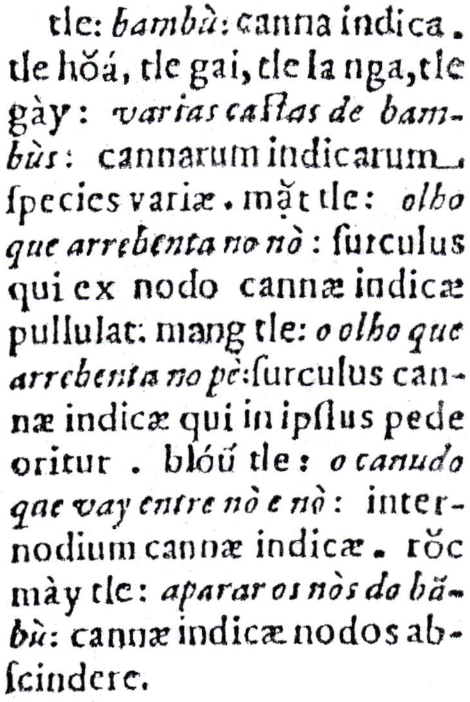

tle: *bambù:* canna indica .
tle hŏá, tle gai, tle la nga, tle
gày: *varias castas de bam-*
bùs: cannarum indicarum,
species variæ. mặt tle: *olho*
que arrebenta no nò: surculus
qui ex nodo cannæ indicæ
pullulat: mang tle: *o olho que*
arrebenta no pé: surculus cannæ indicæ qui in ipsius pede
oritur . blóŭ tle: *o canudo*
que vay entre nò e nò: inter-
nodium cannæ indicæ. rŏc
mày tle: *aparar os nòs do bã-*
bù: cannæ indicæ nodos ab-
scindere.

Figures 2.2–3 (Continued)

alphabet to transcribe indigenous words to evangelize the ancient kingdom of Việt. They invented what is now called "quốc ngữ" – in other words, a means to transcribe the indigenous language through the medium of words written using the Latin alphabet.

"Tre", the name for bamboo that is now the most current, is written **tle**[9] in the *Dictionarium Annamiticum Lusitanum et Latinum* by Alexandre de Rhodes (1651). In this work, all the terms for bamboo, its parts, techniques for use and products made from it are listed. These numerous names prove the multiplicity of uses of the plant, in the 17th century at least, and perhaps even earlier.

In this dictionary,[10] not only **tle** but also several other varieties are mentioned: **tle hóa, tle gai, tle la nga**. There is also a mention of **tle gày** with "canna indica foeminima" as a definition (bamboo "feminine", meaning frail, slender), which is interesting concerning the falsely "sexed" masculine/feminine distinction between bamboo types; solid and dense being considered as "male" (tre đực), and the others with a more hollow and frailer trunk are "female" (tre cái). **Nỗ, tle nỗ**: slender bamboo. Another notable entry: **tlải, tle tlải** "canna indica minutior

22 Bamboo: an anthropological and historical approach

ampla habeus folia" (bamboo of small size with large leaves). Note that **nứa**, a common bamboo, often used for fencing and basket making, is also mentioned as well as: **blóũ nứa** (**nứa** internode), **nan nứa** (**nứa** slat), **đạp** ("đập") **nứa** (to crush **nứa**), **chẻ nứa** (to split **nứa**), **lấy nứa đan phên** (to use **nứa** to weave screens). For **tle** bamboo, we find: **mắttle** (eye of bamboo, meaning the place at a knot where a branch will develop), **blóũ tle** (internode, as written currently: "gióng tre"), **mang tle** (bamboo shoot), **tinh tle** (the whitish powder on the bark of bamboo, compared to seed) and also the expression **róc mày tle** (to lop at the knots on bamboo). Parts of bamboo and products made from bamboo also mentioned by Alexandre de Rhodes: **gốc tle** (the base of bamboo), **mấu tle** (bamboo hook), **đòn gánh** (carrying pole in bamboo), **đũa** (chop sticks), **giàn** (horizontal rack), **giậu** (fence, enclosure), **giỏ** (basket), **lạt** (fine bamboo strip, for basket weaving or tying), **liếp** (fine screen), **lồũ gà** (old written form of "lồng gà", basket for enclosing poultry), **naõ** (old written form of "nong", large flat round basket), **nia** (variation of the previous example), **phên** (closely woven screen in bamboo), **quạt** (or rather "xương quạt", framework for a fan), **rá** (closely woven basket for washing rice), **rèm** (blind in plaited bamboo), **rổ** ("rá"sized bamboo basket, but less closely woven), **sàng** (flat circular basket for riddling rice), **sọt** (basket in varying sizes and weaves), **thúng** (basket).

An erroneous etymology of Bến Tre that some would call "Bamboo loading-dock"

Using an etymology created by the Vietnamese, the *Monographie de la province de Bến Tre*[11] gave the explanation quoted by Vương Hồng Sển: "Bến Tre was once occupied by Cambodians, who named it Sốc Tre (bamboo country) because of the numerous giồng[12] covered in bamboo scattered all over the area. Later on the Annamites established a market that they called Bến Tre (quay in bamboo): the arroyo that flows in front of the market and into the Hàm Luông, bears the same name". Vương Hồng Sển, in his *Dictionnaire du parler méridionnal*, gave the following gloss: in the words Bến Tre, in fact "tre" comes from the Khmer "treay", meaning "fish" because there are still many other place names including fish names in Vietnamese in the region, such as "cầu cá lóc (*Channa striata* bridge)", "cầu cá trê (Catfish bridge)", "Cái Bông (Giant *Channa striata* place)", etc. From this misinterpretation, Vietnamese created a place name in Sino-Vietnamese and Bến Tre became "Trúc Giang (Bamboo Waterway)", whereas it should have been called "Bến Cá (Fish quay)" in Vietnamese, which, in Sino-Vietnamese would be "Ngư Tân". But it had become accepted long ago.[13]

Again, according to this author, the true "bamboo country" is in Biên Hòa province, especially in the villages of Bình Lâm and Thành Tuy Hạ, where not only do many varieties of bamboo grow but also a dozen or so varieties of rattan, whose vernacular names he noted. So, the villages in the area specialize in "basket-ware (nghề đương đát)", particularly in the village of Vĩnh Phước.[14]

Towards the end of the book, Vương Hồng Sển again notes several hilly areas where much bamboo grows (Núi Sa Trúc, Núi Na Sơn), particularly at Núi Lư Duẫn, situated in the north-east of Phước Long district. "Duẫn" means "bamboo". The author notes a variety of bamboo that is much appreciated and typical of Bà Rịa province, called "măng le" ("le" being an earlier form of "tre"; "kle" became "ble", then "tle", then "le", then "tre").[15]

The different parts of the bamboo plant have specific names: "cành tre" are the branches; "lá tre", the leaves. When it is available, "cành tre" makes an excellent whip for cattle; bamboo foliage can be used as quality fodder for water buffalo and oxen.

"Đốt tre" is the internode, also called "gióng tre". It should be noted that internodes become progressively slenderer and shorter the further they are from the base. They appear more "compacted" at the base of the bamboo, where with age they become almost solid, this being known as "tre cật" (a part of bamboo "strong like loins"), "tre đực" (male bamboo), or "tre đặc" (full bamboo). This is the strongest part of the bamboo, chosen for making objects that need to be highly resistant; for example, carrying poles ("đòn gánh"); wood would not be suitable because a carrying pole needs to be light and not crush the shoulder supporting it but resistant enough not to break (a broken carrying pole remains the worst of taboos, synonym of misfortune, breakdown of marriage or death of a partner). The most important quality of a carrying pole is its elasticity: when in use, its movement follows the rhythm of the walker while also boosting the pace. Only the base section of a mature bamboo measuring two metres at most can be used to make this instrument. With little market value, the carrying pole nevertheless remains essential for the daily life of the Vietnamese being used to transport all sorts of supplies but also, when necessary, becoming a formidable defensive weapon. "Mắt, mấu tre" denotes the asperities at the node where the buds that will develop into branches are situated, being compared to an "eye (mắt)" at this stage. In some varieties of bamboo, when they have not yet started to develop into branches, these "eyes" form the "three stars (tam tinh)" that are popular for making staffs of old age.

"Thân tre" is the bamboo trunk, a term that we prefer to the word "culm", even though "culm" is more correct in botanical terms, bamboo being classified as a grass with a hollow stalk, stronger on the outside than on the inside, unlike wood, where the exterior is less resistant than the core.

24 *Bamboo: an anthropological and historical approach*

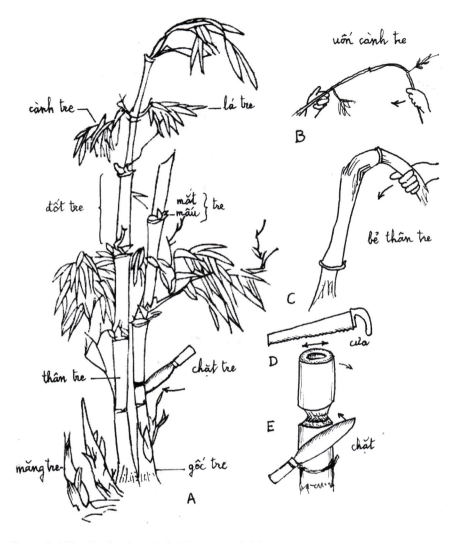

Figure 2.4 Naming bamboo. Left (A): names of different parts of bamboo. Right (B, C, D, E): Appropriating bamboo. Drawings: (1) left (Oger, 1909, p. 206), (2) right by Đinh Trọng Hiếu.

"Măng tre" are the young bamboo shoots growing around the base of the bamboo plant ("gốc tre"). They are cut off using a knife, peeled, boiled to remove some of their natural bitterness and then cooked or stir-fried with pork or poultry.

It is possible to bend a bamboo branch ("uốn cành tre") but difficult to break it neatly ("bẻ thân tre"), even a very slender branch, let alone a bamboo trunk (see Figure 2.4, B, C, D, E). To cut bamboo a tool is essential, preferably a knife ("chặt

Terminology and technology 25

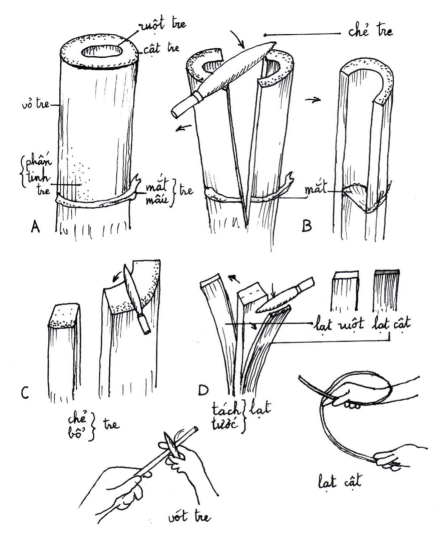

Figure 2.5 Structure of bamboo and related technology. Drawing by Đinh Trọng Hiếu.

tre") or a saw ("cưa tre"). A knife is the preferred tool, as it can be used in many of the different stages: lopping and trimming, cutting down and cutting up.

The branches and the top of the trunk are pliable, and the "springiness" of these parts of the plant is exploited for making traps, particularly for snares; the elasticity of bamboo makes it the irreplaceable, chosen material to trap animals, from tiny birds to large wildlife, from boar to tigers.

After cutting down a bamboo trunk, it then has to be trimmed: its leafy branches must be removed, and then, the irregularities around the knots. This

26 *Bamboo: an anthropological and historical approach*

is what Alexandre de Rhodes' *Dictionarium* called "róc mày tre". The bamboo is then ready to be used, so it is then "prepared (pha tre)" for its different future uses in exactly the same way as a butcher "prepares to make cuts of meat (pha thịt)", once the animal has been slaughtered, cleaned and gutted. This "preparation" of the bamboo takes place in a strict order, each phase having its own terminology dictated by the structure of the bamboo. Inverting the stages poses a problem.

Structure of the bamboo trunk

When cut, a section of the trunk of bamboo reveals that the texture on the outside becomes different towards the core: what is called "vỏ tre" (or improperly "bamboo bark", bamboo not having bark) is smooth, often shiny green in colour, and sometimes dusted with white powder at the knots, powder called "phấn" or "tinh tre" (essential bamboo powder). This outside layer of the "bark" has a somewhat waxy appearance and serves as waterproofing. At the knots, bamboo split in two reveals a diaphragm that is less resistant and can be pierced and/or removed. This layer means a section of a bamboo trunk can be used as a container to carry water. However, all the diaphragms must necessarily be removed from the bamboo trunk intended for use as a water conduit.

From the "bark" inwards, the fibres in the next layer towards the core, observed in cross-section, are dense, close and hard. Strips split from this part of the plant are pliable, resistant and sharp-edged; they form the part called "cật tre" (word for word: the framework giving bamboo its strength), while the internal fibres are lax and spongy. This part is called "ruột tre" (internal, soft, like entrails). A thin, invisible film covers all the inside and is only visible when rice is cooked in a bamboo tube; the rice cooked in this way is held in shape by the film, which resembles tissue paper. It is still present in bamboo that has dried; it adheres to the interior surfaces of the bamboo and determines the sound quality of musical instruments crafted from tubes of bamboo.

Gestures and postures in bamboo work

Bamboo technology is based on the direction of its fibres. Cutting across the fibres ("chặt, đốn, đẵn") is used to separate bamboo from its roots and to cut it into sections. Cutting in the direction of the fibres is much easier, as the saying goes, "easy as splitting bamboo (dễ như chẻ tre)". It goes without saying, "chẻ, fendre" is specific to this action and only used in this context (see Figure 2.5, B and C).

A knife is only necessary to start the first few centimetres of the split; the rest can be done with bare hands. This produces bamboo "rods" with dense fibres on one side and spongy fibres on the other. One only needs to smooth the sides of this rod to obtain a ready-to-use wand. If one needs either wands or strips with a more

Terminology and technology 27

Figures 2.6 Postures while at work: a craftsman making bamboo frame lanterns. Splitting a length of bamboo. Hà Nội. 1979. Photograph by Đinh Trọng Hiếu.

homogenous texture, then the bamboo is given the required thickness by "separating" the fibres ("tách, tước") (see Figure 2.5, D). In this way, two or three sorts of "strips (lạt)" are obtained. One is top quality, from the dense outside fibres; these contain a lot of silica, so the strip remains razor-sharp unless the cutting edge is removed by "smoothing (vót)" it, usually with a knife. This produces "lạt cật", which, as it is pliable, is a favourite material for basket-weaving, is durable and acquires a fine patina. The next strip towards the inside has more spongy fibres that are rich in cellulose and is considered to be medium-quality; it is used alternately with the outside strips as a way to create decorative motifs. Strips from the

28 *Bamboo: an anthropological and historical approach*

Figures 2.7 Postures while at work: a craftsman making bamboo frame lanterns. Sorting the strips of bamboo into outside strips (pliable and strong), and spongy inner strips. Hà Nội. 1979. Photograph by Đinh Trọng Hiếu.

Figure 2.8 Craftsmen preparing strips of bamboo: sitting on low stools, spreading out the material on the ground in front of them. Behind them, note the fine examples of woven bamboo in the screen-panels: French door panel ("liếp") and open-weave panel in bamboo strips ("phên thưa"). *circa* 1923. ANOM. Photograph by Service Photographique du Gouvernement Général de l'Indochine.

Terminology and technology 29

Figure 2.9–10 Ethnic minority basket hod, Central Việt Nam. Basket-ware in alternating bamboo strips, outside strips ("lạt cật") with honey-coloured patina and fibrous inside strips ("lạt ruột") without patina. Paris. 2018. Photograph by Đinh Trọng Hiếu.

30 Bamboo: an anthropological and historical approach

Figures 2.9–10 (Continued)

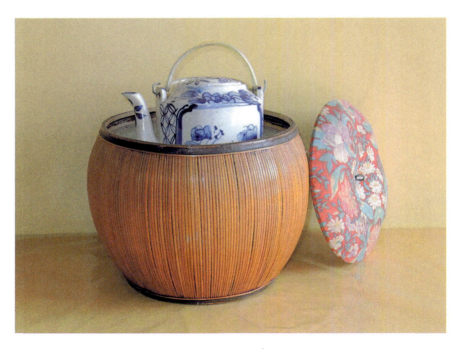

Figures 2.11–12 Two models of teapot baskets ("ấm giành") using outer bamboo strips ("lạt cật") to make products for daily use. Paris. 2018. Photograph by Đinh Trọng Hiếu.

Terminology and technology 31

Figures 2.11–12 (Continued)

inside part of the bamboo ("lạt ruột, inside strips", word-for-word "intestinal") are poor quality but still put to good use. Separated out into fine lengths they make extremely strong ties for all sorts of use without needing to be knotted. A tie will hold just by being twisted around on itself.

Nowadays, especially with the grouping of bamboo craftspeople in "trade villages", many people do not grow bamboo anymore. As they no longer fell or prepare it, they purchase bamboo that is felled and ready to use. They produce a smaller range of items but tend to specialize in one particular item, produce it in large quantities, near the place of sale; in doing so they produce large amounts of

32 *Bamboo: an anthropological and historical approach*

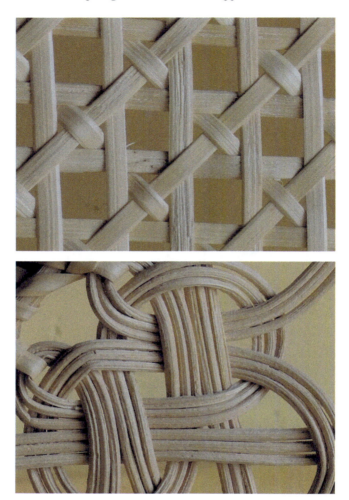

Figures 2.13–14 Use of poor-quality inner strips ("lạt ruột") for decorating everyday objects but with an untidy finish. The decorative effect, however, is clear. Paris. 2018. Photograph by Đinh Trọng Hiếu.

similar waste material, and even though such waste is biodegradable, the concentration of it is becoming a problem.

Notes

1 Nguyễn Quang Hồng, 2008, p. 110 sq.
2 The so-called "Hán-Việt" pronunciation is that of the Chinese vocabulary introduced in large quantities into spoken Vietnamese in the 10th and 11th centuries.

Terminology and technology   33

3 The so-called "phi Hán-Việt" pronunciation is that of the Chinese vocabulary introduced sporadically into spoken Vietnamese either before the 10th and 11th centuries or following this period.

4 The character 房 was pronounced "phòng" in Hán-Việt.

5 口, a Chinese radical used as a diacritical mark in "nôm", cannot be considered as a creation. In fact, it is an example of a borrowed sinogram. Thus, 咦 ("gì"), which in Vietnamese means "what, that", is borrowed from a character 咦 ("yí") expressing surprise in Chinese.

6 In the absence of the mark, the reading of the character 某 was unclear. It could be pronounced "mỗ" (sv.) or "mỏ" (vn.).

7 "呐荽呐蘱,業呬庄嫌所薿荄 Ăn rau ăn blái (trái), nghiệp miệng chăng (chẳng) hèm (hiềm) thửa đẳng cay (If one eats vegetables and fruit, the mouth does not reject bitter and spicey flavours)", *Cư trần lạc đạo phú* 居塵樂道賦 in Nguyễn Huệ Chi, 1989, vol. 3, p. 498.

8 It even appears in two different forms– 知, 楲– in the dictionary *Chỉ nam ngọc âm giải nghĩa*. 指南玉音解義. The reader will find examples for each of these characters in the dictionaries compiled by Nguyễn Hữu Vinh and Nguyễn Quang Hồng (Nguyễn Hữu Vinh et al., 2009, p. 1351; Nguyễn Quang Hồng, 2015, vol. 2, pp. 1919–20). See also *infra*, Chapter 4, p. 63. It should be noted that 雯, which is included in Oger's list, is not present in dictionaries in vernacular writing.

9 Other examples of the transformation of "tl" to "tr": "tlái" > "trái" (fruit), "tlời" > "trời" (sky), often via "bl": "blái, blời", a form which does not occur for "tle"; "nôm" also presents a similar transition as shown in the example of 蘱 "blái" mentioned above.

10 The words concerning bamboo found in Alexandre de Rhodes' *Dictionarium* are in bold in this paragraph.

11 The *Monographie de la province de Bến Tre* was published by the Société des Études Indochinoises, Librairie Ménard, 1903.

12 "banks".

13 Vương Hồng Sển, 1993, p. 151.

14 *Ibidem*, p. 176.

15 *Ibidem*, p. 745.

3 Uses of bamboo according to its qualities

Yves Crouzet, once the director of the Bambouseraie d'Anduze, has written a short book that we highly recommend: *Travailler le bambou*. He mentions the meticulous work of Willard Porterfield in 1933, which identifies up to 1,546 uses for bamboo for Japan alone. Rather than selecting from this inventory those that have fallen into disuse – which would be a pity because the memory of the past might then be lost – or adding other uses still current in Việt Nam or elsewhere in the world, we decided to make a tour of the uses of bamboo according to its qualities and its cut. The qualities and the properties of the plant depend on the variety, where it grows and its age. The uses are listed according to the number of procedures necessary, starting with those where there are none, the bamboo being used as it is, the only procedure having been to plant it knowingly and to nurture it.

In this chapter, the uses of the bamboo as a living plant will be analyzed; then bamboo felled, with no other processing; then bamboo cut into lengths (for uses such as tubes and pipes). A second section describes the purposes for bamboo cut into rods and strips. The main sub-products obtained will be considered, such as those in basket-ware, bearing in mind that there are in fact a countless number of sub-products!

Bamboo as a living plant

The military and defensive use of bamboo in Việt Nam is both ancient and widespread. The *Complete Book of the Historical Records of Đại Việt* already mentioned the plantation of thorny bamboo ("thứ trúc" 刺竹) as a green fence[1] in 858 in Giao Châu. However, the earliest reference to such use appears in *Categorized Sayings from the library* by Lê Quý Đôn:

> In his *Treatise on Bamboo* [Zhupu 竹譜], Dai Kaizhi 戴凱之 [Jin dynasty, 266–420] writes that thorny bamboo ("jizhu" 棘竹) grows closely and thickly, a small thicket is like a forest. [. . .] It is also called "bazhu/ba trúc 笆竹, hedge bamboo", as an enclosure it is very sturdy. Note: thorny bamboo grows at all the commanderies of Jiaozhou, the largest trunks have a diameter of two feet.[2]

Uses of bamboo according to its qualities 35

Figure 3.1 Bamboo hedge surrounding a dwelling, seen from inside. Đông Hồ Village. Bắc Ninh Province. 1982. Photograph by Đinh Trọng Hiếu.

Until the colonial period and during the modern era, many villages in the north of Việt Nam were still surrounded by thorny bamboo hedges as protection against pirates and thieves. Nowadays, some villages still retain intact lengths of the vestiges of these hedges, notably in the village of Đào Xá (in the Midland Region), as shown by the raised bank still visible on the photograph taken in 1982 (see Figure 3.2). Indeed, in order to clearly limit the extent of the village, here we can see young bamboo and their rhizomes have been planted on banks roughly one metre in height, so that the young plants do not grow in all directions and can quickly establish a new dense hedge.

Village people, however, have always taken one precaution: as bamboo tends to grow in a south-westerly direction, the hedge must be planned so that it does not progress towards the centre of the village. This process must have been known for long time as it was described by Lê Quý Đôn in the 18th century, quoting a Chinese source from the time of the Tang dynasty, the *Zhong shu shu* 種樹書 [Treatise on arboriculture] by Guo Tuotuo 郭橐駝: "Bamboo likes to grow in the direction of the south west[3]".

Use of cut bamboo

A length of bamboo that has just been cut and whose extremities are sealed by the diaphragms behaves like a tube corked at both ends: it floats.

This attribute of bamboo has been used by generations of inhabitants of the Red River delta for the transport of felled bamboo (particularly the "nứa" variety), from

36 *Bamboo: an anthropological and historical approach*

Figure 3.2 Double bamboo hedge, Đào Xá Village. Right, bamboo growing in the village hedge, on a bank. Left, bamboo hedge of a dwelling, Đào Xá Village. Phú Thọ Province. 1982. Photograph by Đinh Trọng Hiếu.

Uses of bamboo according to its qualities 37

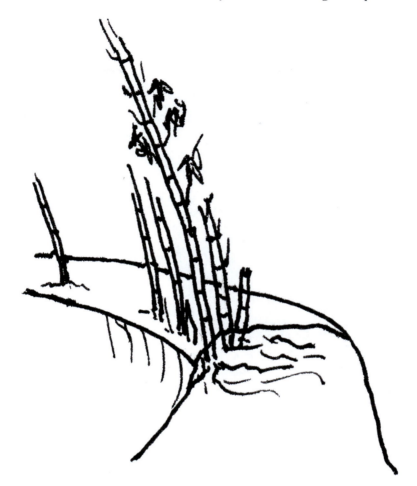

Figure 3.3 Planting young bamboo on a bank. Drawing by Đinh Trọng Hiếu.

the forested areas of the Highlands in northern Việt Nam by creating large "rafts" called "bè nứa" and drifting them down the long rivers to their destination. During the Tonkin campaign (1884), Doctor Hocquard observed this practice, then appropriated it for military use:

> This time we are crossing the Black River on a fine bamboo bridge built by our military engineers. The bridge is installed in an innovative fashion: at the present moment bamboo rafts covered with bundles of the dried palm leaves used in the delta to thatch huts, come down from the furthest reaches of the

38 *Bamboo: an anthropological and historical approach*

Figure 3.4 Simple raft of bamboo trunks tied together. ANOM. Photograph by Service Photographique du Gouvernement Général de l'Indochine.

Black River to join the Red River for landing at Hanoï. We have intercepted a great number of these rafts which have been placed end to end by joining them together with cross beams made of bunches of bamboo; and thus produced a good strong pontoon bridge. Rattan cables, which the Annamites use to tow their boats, have been strung across the river from one bank to the other; they immobilise the bridge and prevent it from drifting away[4].

Uses of bamboo according to its qualities 39

Figure 3.5 Bamboo rafts used by French military engineers as a pontoon bridge to cross the Black River, 1884. ANOM. Photograph by Charles-Edouard Hocquard.

Concurrently, but very differently, bamboo was being used as a means of obstruction on navigable waterways in the central region. This was the work of Trần Tiễn Thành and his colleague Nguyễn Như Thăng "who set up [. . .] between the forts of Qui Lai and Thuận Hòa and the place known as Cồ Cò Xứ, lines of bamboo staves forming barrages to defend the channel against enemy gunships, with the provision at the centre of a gap of 2.5 metres for the passage of the royal junks. They also made preparations on each bank, opposite the villages of Qui Lai and Thuận Hòa, for bamboo rafts (each being 100 stems) to be pushed to the middle of the river in the case of alert, and on each side of the river, for depositing at the same spot, piles of stones, to be used if needed, to block the channel".[5]

Lengths of bamboo cut to retain a diaphragm and then used as containers

In order to go and draw water from a source and bring it back home, villagers use a length of bamboo retaining a diaphragm at one end, choosing one of the varieties with long internodes, as this makes for a container with a greater capacity. Usually the variety called "bương" (*Gigantochloa levis*) is chosen, its diameter being wide and its internodes, long. Carrying is very simple: either a cord is tied round the bamboo and used as a shoulder strap or the cords are strung over a carrying pole in order to carry several containers at the same time.

In old Việt Nam, bamboo simply cut into sections could be used to enclose correspondence to be carried by courier. This use is noted here and will be developed

40 *Bamboo: an anthropological and historical approach*

Figure 3.6 Lengths of bamboo obturated at one end by its diaphragm and used for carrying water without any additional procedure. Cao Bằng. *Circa* 1940. ANOM, Photograph by Service Photographique du Gouvernement Général de l'Indochine.

in the chapter concerning bamboo and its relations to power. The same applies to bamboo used as a cangue to punish or constrain convicts.

Lengths of bamboo used in waterwheels as water containers

Waterwheels are an important part of the irrigation system in Việt Nam. The *Imperially Commissioned Itemized Summaries of the Comprehensive Mirror of Việt History* reports that, in 1687, because of a long drought and a sudden rise in the cost of rice, the court instructed mandarins from the capital to visit the provinces in order to examine the configuration of the terrain, and according to their observations, to order waterwheels ("thủy xa" 水車) to be built for irrigating the rice fields.[6] The lengths of bamboo fixed to the wheel need little human intervention, but the construction of a waterwheel requires extensive knowledge of its mechanism. The workings of a small waterwheel can be clearly divided into four stages:

- Bamboo dippers scoop the water (making the dippers is the only stage requiring a simple procedure).
- The bamboo dippers are carried up and around by the wheel.
- The water tips from the dippers into a conduit.
- The water runs along the conduit to its destination.[7]

Uses of bamboo according to its qualities 41

Figure 3.7 Gigantochloa levis ("bương") is often chosen for its long internodes. Hòa Bình. 2003. Photograph by Vũ Thế Long.

Bamboo trunks felled and used as they are for building (roof structures or scaffolding)

Several precautions must be taken in the selection process for these purposes: first of all, the chosen bamboo must be at least four years old, in a variety that has a

42 *Bamboo: an anthropological and historical approach*

strong trunk with a full core, known as "male bamboo" (no sexual connotation). Felling must be carried out during the dry, cool season to avoid the accumulation of nourishing substances in the fibres that could attract insects. In the past, soaking in mud for one or more years was carried out, followed by a long drying period in the shade.

Figure 3.8 A large waterwheel in the Highland region in the north. *Circa* 1930. Photograph by Gouvernement Général de l'Indochine, published in Albert Sarraut, 1930. p. 42.

Uses of bamboo according to its qualities 43

Figure 3.9 Waterwheels in Quảng Ngãi (Central Việt Nam). ANOM. DAFANCAOM.

Figure 3.10–11 Bamboo roof structure in Thanh Hà Village; holes are bored through the trunks used as pillars. Thanh Hà Village. Vĩnh Phúc Province. 1989. Photograph by Đinh Trọng Hiếu.

44 *Bamboo: an anthropological and historical approach*

Figures 3.10–11 (Continued)

Figure 3.12 Bamboo used for mounting a swing. "Inauguration du Grand Bouddha: la balançoire". Hà Nội, Quán Thánh temple. 1893. Bibliothèque numérique d'Université Côte d'Azur. Photograph by Schneider.

Uses of bamboo according to its qualities 45

Figure 3.13 Bamboo used for scaffolding at Cổ Loa. Hà Nội Province. 1995. Photograph by Đinh Trọng Hiếu.

46　*Bamboo: an anthropological and historical approach*

Methods for preserving bamboo

Soaking

The *vulgum pecus* refers to the bamboo stalk as "trunk" by analogy with trees, rather than "culm", the word used by botanists, which is more correct, for bamboo belongs to the extensive family of *Graminae*: the structure of "culm" being the opposite of wood, being dense on the outside and soft on the inside. But this would surprise the Vietnamese user, who is more likely to identify bamboo by size and strength, being more inclined to assimilate it with a tree and its "trunk" rather than with a grass and its "culm".

The structure of bamboo means that it is more vulnerable than wood because its fibres are rich in cellulose, starch and sugars. Such substances are easily degradable, particularly when bamboo is used as a building material resting in the ground in humid conditions. Insects are also attracted to these substances, so that bamboo used for construction purposes lasts little more than four to five years. In order to overcome these problems, traditional methods of preservation are used.

Bamboo used for building purposes must first be soaked ("ngâm tẩm") immediately after harvesting. Immersion in pond water must be complete so that the trunks are completely covered by the mud ("ngâm bùn"); if necessary, they are weighed down with stones to keep them under the water because bamboo floats. This operation lasts one to three years, and in the past, could last up to ten years because this treatment of the material appreciably extends the life of the building. When the bamboo is removed from its mud bath, it stinks, so it has to be left to dry and lose some of its unpleasant odour. The drying process must be carried out in the shade and not in the sun, which could make the trunk split. Often, someone entering a new house built with bamboo that has been treated in this way is struck by the terrible smell that can last for years. However, the odour is the sign of a quality material because bamboo that has lost all the starch from its fibres no longer attracts parasites and is more resistant to bad weather or other risks. The unpleasant odour remaining after maceration is harmless for the inhabitants.

Concerning the felling of bamboo and the harvesting of bamboo shoots in the south of Việt Nam, Vương Hồng Sển notes that: "this work must be undertaken while there is no moon. Moonlight encourages attacks from insects".[8]

Smoking

Bamboo that has been cut for making basket-ware is not treated by maceration in mud. It is worked raw, as soon as it is cut, with no preliminary drying period so that the strips remain pliable. But the product, once it is finished, is smoked ("hun khói"). Traditionally, this is a slow process, the finished objects being simply placed above the hearth. After a while (depending on the amount of smoke created by cooking), the bamboo becomes a more-or-less-pronounced honey colour. A piece that has been given this slow treatment can eventually acquire a fine patina through use called "lên nước". If the piece has been made with the outside part of the bamboo, as the material dries, it becomes both more pliable and more resistant. If it has been made with the fibrous inside part, it is not smoked because these products do not need such treatment, as they are made for use inside or are intended to be temporary (partition, fence). Nowadays, in order to give a good patina to basket-ware, smoke machines are used, a treatment intended to extend the life of objects. For walking sticks, fishing rods and other poles in full bamboo or tube form bamboo, smoking must be very slow and carefully observed because too much or too sudden a heat risks splitting the bamboo, which would render it useless.

Bamboo to be used for building should be felled in winter. In the spring, rapid growth produces fibres that are less resistant and too rich in the substances that attract insects. Chemical products used at present to "treat" bamboo are not mentioned here.

Use as a vessel for cooking

Many of the ethnic minorities in the Highlands in the north of Việt Nam cook sticky rice in a length of freshly cut bamboo about 5 centimetres in diameter, where one end is closed by the diaphragm. Usually "dang" or "giang" (*Dendrocalamus*) bamboo is selected with sides that are not too thick so that the rice cooks easily and quickly. A layer of the outside bark is removed if it is too thick. The tube is filled three-quarters full with washed rice; the remaining quarter is filled to the top with water and the open end is carefully sealed with a crumpled banana leaf. The tube is placed in the fire or on hot coals, taking care that the tube does not char through as it would if the bamboo were not freshly cut: sap seeps from the tube and sizzles gently. When the tube begins to blacken and the sizzling ceases, it is removed from the hearth and the tube is removed by carefully splitting it. A long cylinder of cooked sticky rice is revealed, wrapped in a fine, translucent film, the vestige of the membrane lining the bamboo. As it cooks, the rice absorbs the sap from the freshly cut bamboo, giving it a delicious, distinctive taste. This is how "cơm lam" (sticky rice cooked in a bamboo tube) is prepared. Pork or poultry can be cooked in the same way as long as the meat has been finely minced, bamboo not being resistant to fierce heat or too long a cooking time.

Walking sticks, knife handles

Here, the right choice of the variety is essential. Those most favoured are the diminutive yellow bamboos called "trúc", and among these, preference goes to "trúc đùi

Figure 3.14 Staff of Old Age made from "chicken leg" bamboo with the "three stars" at each internode. Đào Xá. 1982. Photograph by Đinh Trọng Hiếu.

gà" ("trúc" chicken legs), for the internodes are plump and yellow in colour, like a chicken's legs, or "trúc hóa long" ("trúc" metamorphosed into a dragon, with at the base of the trunk, strangely shaped internodes). Generally, this is the variety *Phyllostachys bambusoides* Sieb. et Zucc., and other varieties in the same family such as *aurea* (Carr. ex Rib.) Mak. that has multiple nuances of shape and colour. The main criterion for selection is the thickness of the outer layer: bamboo chosen for a walking stick or a tool handle should be thick or even full, so that it does not split or crack. Another very important consideration is aesthetic, the favoured selection being dictated by traditional beliefs or personal preference. At each internode, the "three stars (tam tinh)", the place where three branch buds join, must be carefully removed as soon as they form. Such a walking stick, or "staff of old age", is the envy of all the elders, and the bamboo specimen discovered in a clump is carefully tended and cut only when it has grown to the required length (multiple of the number six, counting the internodes: "Sinh, Lão, Bệnh, Khổ, Tử", "Birth, Old Age, Illness, Suffering, Death" starting again with "Birth"). Then this length of bamboo is felled, straightened, cut, polished and tended. The choice of plant to be used for canes, sticks, umbrella handles and so on depends on similar criteria.

Fishing rods

On the other hand, a fishing rod must not be rigid. Often, *Phyllostachys nigra* (Lodd.) Munro, var. *henonis* (Milf.) Stapf ex Rendle, called "trúc cần câu" ("trúc" variety for fishing rods) is chosen not only for pliability but also for its gradually

Uses of bamboo according to its qualities 49

Figure 3.15 Knife handle made from full straight bamboo with the "three stars" at each internode. Đào Xá. 1982. Photograph by Đinh Trọng Hiếu.

tapering diameter. The rod must be thick enough to be held comfortably in the hand but taper gradually towards the top to provide the necessary pliability for teasing the bait and hooking the fish. However, the rod must also be strong enough to support the weight of the catch without breaking.

Sound quality: musical instruments

The criteria for external attributes of a particular bamboo to be used for making a musical instrument are different to those mentioned earlier. Bamboo selected for its sound quality, as we have already seen, depends partly on the membrane covering the inside of the plant and partly on its silica content. The bamboo selected for each type of instrument requires certain adjustments to give a chosen segment the relevant shape and to improve its sound quality. Usually, the Vietnamese choose "trúc" bamboo to make end-blown or side-blown flutes with the result that music played on such instruments is called "(tiếng trúc) bamboo music", indicating the material used, whereas music played on instruments with silk strings is called "(tiếng tơ) silk music". So here "trúc" has become synonymous with "flute". Later, we will see that there are many other musical instruments made with bamboo that are neither wind nor stringed. There are also percussion instruments or idiophones and those with other sorts of strings made from bamboo bark. Here are some examples:

- Wind instruments such as end-blown or side-blown flutes, with or without holes, used by the Vietnamese for learned music and/or folk music.

- Percussion instruments, and generally, we will give a brief description of those invented by the various ethnic minorities in Central Việt Nam who choose to use "nứa" (type *Neohouzeaua*, or *Schizostachyum*) bamboo as the base material. It has two useful characteristics: its trunk contains a considerable amount of silica providing a percussion instrument with a "metallic" (or "crystalline") sound, and also, a fine layer of the "bark" can be detached to form a sort of "vibrating string".

Why is bamboo sharp? The uses of this property

As noted earlier, a bamboo trunk has a very strong, hard cortical outer layer where the fibres have high silica content and a softer spongy inner part. When bamboo is cut into rods, an edge of the outer dense "cortical" layer of fibre can be bevelled (Figure 3.15, edge AB). This edge is necessarily sharp, like a razor blade. As all bamboo has a similar general structure, depending on the way it is cut, it can always be sharp. There is, however, a "rule" for detecting which bamboo is sharper than others because the sharpest resonates the best. The greater the silica content in bamboo, the more it resonates (like crystal), a property inherent to silica (like a shard of glass). But, although resonance is consubstantial in bamboo, its cutting properties result from how it is felled and cut. This property is however ephemeral, as the cutting edge of bamboo wears away rapidly or can be quickly removed with a knife, an operation called "vót tre" ("smoothing bamboo").

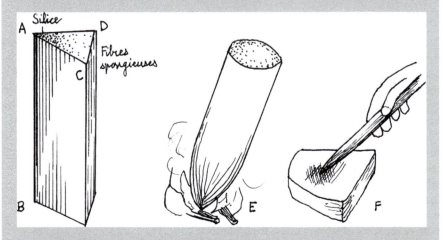

Figure 3.16 The cutting edge of a bamboo blade: edge AB is the cortical layer of a bamboo trunk. Hardening a bamboo point on a fire (E). 3. Polishing on a stone (F). Drawings by Đinh Trọng Hiếu.

Because "nứa" bamboo has the best resonance, it is the preferred variety for making musical instruments, particularly for percussion. It is also the sharpest and can easily be split in two. Artisans who work with bamboo must have calloused hands or they would easily cut themselves when manipulating it. One of the cruellest tortures in the 19th century was to slide a convict between blades of razor-sharp "nứa" ("tuốt nứa"). To build a fence around a house, this bamboo is cut in half lengthways and stuck into the ground. These vertical poles are then consolidated halfway up with other trunks split in two, and the verticals are then shaped to a point with a knife. In the mountainous areas, it is said that tigers, by instinct, prefer not to jump over these fences, not because they can't but because they know how "nứa" can cut: the blades would not necessarily cause deadly wounds but even a slight cut from "nứa" – with the tiger then licking it with his rough tongue – could become infected and leave the tiger unable to hunt. This is how a tiger, which does not usually eat human flesh, becomes "anthropophagic", as there is no easier prey for a wounded tiger than a human being, especially if attacked from behind. The carnivore then gradually develops mange from a diet that has become too rich in salt (see Figure 3.17).

The sharp quality of "nứa" is also used at a birth. Small blades of this bamboo were used to cut the umbilical cord because a metal blade was not considered suitable and, if used, the new baby often died of tetanus.

Figure 3.17 The dry fence on the right protects against incursion from a tiger. Cabaton, 1932, p. 95.

> Kitchen use of little bamboo blades is more appropriate for slicing the intestines of poultry in order to avoid the "smell of cold fish (tanh)" that would emanate from offal in contact with metal.
>
> Nowadays, the sharpness of bamboo is still put to use for building barriers of stakes around villages. To sharpen the stakes – in the same way as arrows are made – the ends can be heated over a fire, then smoothed and polished on a stone (see Figure 3.16, F).
>
> The sharpness of this bamboo has been known for centuries: the *Nanfang Caomu Zhuang* 南方草木狀 by Ji Han (4th century CE) mentions it in these terms: "The 'shi lin zhu 石林竹' [Stone Forest bamboo] resembles 'cinnamon bamboo'. It is strong and sharp. It is shaped to make knives that can cut elephant hide as easily as taro. It grows in Jiuren (Cửu Chân) and in Jiaozhi (Giao Chỉ)".[9]

Trimming bamboo tubes to different sizes means they then provide different notes; hanging from a double cord, they are played with two wooden sticks, producing a crystalline sound. This is "đàn t'rưng" music, notably played by the Rhade ethnic minority.[10] Other ethnic groups from the Highlands also play this popular instrument, which is mentioned later in the context of the performances of a young musician from the Bahnar ethnic group in Kontum.

Other "nứa" bamboo tubes are adequately adjusted and trimmed and held in one hand (or both) and struck on a wooden block or on ceramic slabs, producing metallic sounds. This is the "đing pâng" Rhade (Êđê) ethnic group.

The Rhade reproduce the sound of gongs by using wooden sticks to play on tubes of this same bamboo. Known as "ching kram" (or "gong bamboo"), it is played by groups at Buôn Ma Thuột. Performances of most of these instruments have been filmed, and the reader may choose to consult video and sound recordings to see how the instruments are made and to learn about the production of this "green music".

Few instruments are as simple as the "pah pung" (also called "klong put"), but making one clearly requires good knowledge of the structure of bamboo to make the tubes resonate with the movement of air. Unequal lengths of "nứa" are laid out flat on the ground or slightly raised on a support. The difference in length is achieved, if necessary, by puncturing the diaphragm at the internodes and is calculated to produce a different note for each tube in respect of the tuning of the ensemble. It can be classed as a wind instrument, even though it is not blown. The player uses her hands to produce the sound. With the instrument laid horizontally in front of her with her hands slightly cupped towards the front, she claps her hands to send a puff of wind into the chosen tube, producing a different sound for each tube. Different notes are produced according to the length and the diameter of the bamboo. Several "pah pung" players can perform together in concert. This unusual

Uses of bamboo according to its qualities 53

Figure 3.18 Percussion instruments "đing pâng" made of bamboo tubes. This percussion can also be performed on a wooden block as in Buôn Ma Thuột. 2017. *Screen shot.* Available: www.vinaculto.vn/vn/news/79/detail/747/trung-bay-trien-lam-va-trinh-dien- tre-nua-trong-doi-song-am-nhac-dan-toc-viet-nam.aspx [Accessed: 21/03/2020].

polyphonic music is pleasant and gentle to the ear. The Rhade ethnic group in the Central Highlands play the "pah pung" and recordings exist from 1955.[11]

The instrument, called "đàn tập tình" ("tập tình" musical instrument), is a tube zither also made from a length of the same "nứa" bamboo. Making this apparently simple instrument requires great dexterity, as it involves detaching the fibres, without breaking them, from the "cortical" part of the bamboo so that they can be transformed into "strings", each resting on a bridge placed under each one.[12]

This instrument is played by plucking the "strings" or by hitting them with a small stick, in the manner of the mountain people of the Central Highlands (recordings by Mission Frantz Laforest in 1955) and also the Tày (Thái) ethnic group in Nghệ An Province.[13]

The last example in our study is an exceptional instrument: the "water chimes" (or "tang koa") of the Sedang, an ethnic minority in the Central Highlands. The complexity of this instrument can be better apprehended via the concept of Land Art, by its position in the landscape and its ethnic context, although it is not devoid of usefulness. Running water provides the power to activate the instrument's ingenious mechanism. Hammers attached with lianas to the machinery strike the bamboo tubes hanging from a supporting frame, also made of bamboo. Continuous music is the result; both a hymn to the gods and to Nature but also a protection

54 *Bamboo: an anthropological and historical approach*

Figure 3.19 The "pah pung" (or "klong put"). Central Highlands of Việt Nam. Photograph by Laforest printed on the cover of the disk. Laforest, 1955.

from wild animals who might intrude and destroy crops. Jean-Dominique Lajoux (who took the following photographs) gives a full description of the instrument.[14]

"The 'tang koa' has between 20 and 100 sounding tubes producing different notes, but each musical phrase played may include twice that number of notes because some of the tubes are struck by two different hammers during each phase of the to-and-fro swinging movement of the lianas that carry the hammers. Sometimes, the installation is even more complex in that the high notes played by the percussion of small hammers suspended from shorter lianas can be repeated two or three times by rebound on the 'to' movement and similarly on the 'from' movement. By using and combining all these possibilities, the Sedang have learned to build an automatic instrument that plays continuously. Set up by streams and arroyos, the 'tang koa' can be heard from afar in the wooded hills and valleys".[15] In the museum at Đà Nẵng, there is a small-scale working model of the water chime: the visitor is able to observe the instrument as it plays and listen to its music.

Uses of bamboo according to its qualities 55

Figure 3.20 Suspended sound tubes struck by hammers activated by a waterfall ("tang koa"). Unspecified location. Lajoux, 1977, pp. 80–1.

Uses of bamboo after crushing

Crushing bamboo is a simple operation. Practised in the right way using a hammer and chisel, a single length of bamboo can be crushed and transformed into a hammock by weaving in a few cross-strips. The fibres of the bamboo must first be separated in the middle of the trunk, while retaining its initial cylindrical shape at both ends. The fibres that have been spread out by crushing are maintained in place by other strips of bamboo that are woven through the middle part as in basket-ware. The result is a hammock made of a single bamboo trunk that can bear the weight of two small children.

To make a floor covering, a bamboo trunk is partly split using a chisel; then, by breaking the diaphragms that hold the plant in its original cylindrical shape,

Figure 3.21 Two infants sitting in a crushed bamboo hammock, hanging from a bamboo beam. The partition is made of woven bamboo and the floor covering is made from several crushed bamboo trunks placed side by side. Inside a Mường home, in Hòa Bình. 1989. Photograph by Đinh Trọng Hiếu.

Figure 3.22 A bent bamboo trunk that does not break and provides a corner for a strong barrier that is easy to install. However, to bend the bamboo, considerable pressure must be applied even to this type of bamboo with relatively thin bark. Thanh Hà Village. Vĩnh Phúc Province. 1989. Photograph by Đinh Trọng Hiếu.

Uses of bamboo according to its qualities 57

Figure 3.23 "Bẫy cần đánh chim" (snare trap to catch birds). Oger, 1909, p. 438.

the artisan can flatten the trunk while maintaining the strips. A number of bamboo trunks split in this way are used to floor living quarters. With time and use, this bamboo flooring acquires a lovely, shiny, yellowish patina.

Using the spring effect of bamboo branches

After pruning, the slim branches are not thrown away or wasted. They are useful either for mending and reinforcing a basket or their springy quality is put into use

58 *Bamboo: an anthropological and historical approach*

for setting traps. It is not necessary for the branch to be as thick as the branch of a tree in order to remain resistant when bent because bamboo branches are very pliable and do not break under strain. They can be used as springs in most types of snares: this is how small birds can be trapped and larger animals (pheasants, foxes and rabbits) can also be caught in the same way. The pliability of bamboo preserves the animal's limbs, which are not broken by the trap. In most cases, thanks to the gentler trigger mechanism of pliable bamboo, when caught, the animal is not strangled either, but in most cases, stays alive.

On the ground, on flat stones or on a branch, a bird-trap has been placed with a fat worm (or fruit) as bait. Around the trap, a slipknot connects with a spring made of a nicely supple bamboo branch. The bird is attracted by the bait and lands on the bird trap to peck at the bait; in doing so, it sets off the mechanism and the spring is freed, rising and pulling on the slipknot, which closes around the bird's foot.

Notes

1 *TT*, ngoại kỷ, q. V, f ° 8b.
2 Dai Kaizhi, *Zhupu* 竹譜, Waseda edition, ms. 14–00807, f°s 3b-4a. *VĐNL*, q. IX, f ° 72a. The translation of this quotation is from the original version because Lê Quý Đôn's translation is slightly distorted because the scholar had relied on secondary works.
3 *VĐLN*, q. IX, f ° 72b.
4 Hocquard, 1892, p. 162.
5 Đào Duy Anh, 1944, p. 107.
6 *Khâm định Việt sử thông giám cương mục* 欽定越史通鑑綱目, 1884, *chính biên*, q. 34, f ° 19b. Ms. 0174-19 in *The Vietnamese Preservation Nôm Foundation*. Available: https://lib.nomfoundation.org/collection/1/volume/269/ [Accessed: 15/04/2021]. There is also a drawing of a waterwheel by Phạm Thận Duật in his *Brief description of Hưng Hóa* [Hưng Hóa ký lược 興化記略 – 1856] in *Phạm Thận Duật toàn tập* (2000), p. 662.
7 Available: http://giadinh.net.vn/xa-hoi/sung-sung-coi-xay-gio-cua-don-quixote-o-tay-bac-20110623111440682.htm [Accessed: 19/03/2020].
8 Vương Hồng Sển, 1993, p. 633.
9 Ji Han, 1979, p. 134.
10 There are "đàn t'rưng" recordings by Mission Frantz Laforest (1955).
11 There are "pah pung" (or "khlong put") recordings by Mission Frantz Laforest (1955).
12 Available: https://baonghean.vn/xem-nghe-nhan-nguoi-thai-che-tac-nhac-cu-doc-dao-tu-cay-nua-post153988.html [Accessed: 2/02/2020].
13 There are "đàn tập tình" recordings by Mission Frantz Laforest (1955).
14 Lajoux, 1977. Recordings of "tang koa" (or "water chimes") were made by Mission Frantz Laforest in 1955 and by Jean-Dominique Lajoux.
15 Lajoux, 1977, p. 80.

4   Bamboo as symbol

In Việt Nam, as in other countries, there has always been interaction between popular and elite cultures, as shown notably in the writings of the scholars Nguyễn Trãi and Lê Quý Đôn. As a result, the symbolism of bamboo tends to be somewhat ambiguous, oscillating continuously between Nature and Culture. Sometimes valued positively (representing rectitude and self-control), bamboo is also described negatively (as too common and widespread). This symbolism varies according to historical and literary sources but also appears in surveys of attitudes in popular culture.

In works of state historiography, according to a Confucian perspective, bamboo takes pride of place when selecting a symbol for the gentleman, the civilized man ("quân tử" 君子) compared with the inferior man ("tiểu nhân" 小人). As shown in the episode recorded in the *Complete Book of the Historical Records of Đại Việt*, narrating a diplomatic mission to China at the beginning of the 14th century:

> The Year Mậu Thân (1308), 16th [of the Hưng Long era] during the reign of Anh Tông of the Trần, Year 1 of the Zhi Da era in the reign of Wuzong-Haishan of the Yuan. [The Vietnamese ambassador] Mạc Đĩnh Chi, who was a small man, was mocked by the Mongols. One day the Mongol Prime Minister called him to the audience chamber, at about the time of the 5th or 6th moon. Hanging on the chamber wall there was a silk scroll painting of a yellow sparrow perched on a bamboo branch. When Đĩnh Chi pretended to catch the sparrow as if it were a real bird, the Mongols burst out laughing, taking him for an uncouth foreigner. Đĩnh Chi tore down the scroll and threw it on the floor: taking his hosts by surprise. He told them: our elders always painted sparrows perched on the branch of an apricot tree, but never on bamboo as on your scroll. Bamboo represents the gentleman; the sparrow represents the inferior man. With this painting, the Prime Minister appears to be favouring the inferior man at the expense of the civilised man, and in doing so he is in danger of strengthening the former at the expense of the latter. In the name of your venerable Court, I am ready to assist you in eliminating these inferior men.[1]

It should be noted that the Vietnamese ambassador uses dialectics with skill, and while appearing to be an inferior man uncouth in diplomacy, he is nevertheless

DOI: 10.4324/9781003350347-6

defending the cultural value of bamboo and the gentleman. In scholarly culture, bamboo is also a metaphor for longevity, as it stays green in winter. With the two other plants that do not fear the rigours of winter, the evergreen pine tree and the prunus that flowers at the end of winter, it forms the group of "the three cold weather friends" (Suihan sanyou/Tuế hàn tam hữu 歲寒三友). This symbol is omnipresent in Vietnamese culture: some 3 tiền gold and silver coins from the time of the Nguyễn emperors, from Thiệu Trị to Đông Khánh, bear the image of bamboo next to pine and prunus with the words Tam thọ 三壽, "the three longevities".[2]

In the field of Vietnamese and Chinese literary allusions, the symbol of bamboo is a complex one, particularly in the pair formed by the two plants "zhu mei (trúc mai)". While there is no variation either in the graphic or the meaning of "zhu (trúc)" in the texts – 竹–, those of "mei (mai)" are liable to variation and so present a problem. Written 媒 and placed before the word "zhu (trúc) 竹" in "mei zhu (mai trúc)", the word "mei (mai)" has the sense "by means of" and refers to the vow of union expressed by means of a bamboo leaf. So, in the collection of writings by Liang Shaoren 梁紹壬 (1792-?), titled *Liang ban qiu yu an sui bi* 兩般秋雨盦隨筆 [Random Jottings from Autumnal Rain Studio in Two Categories] (from two vases for autumn rain), a boy and girl who had fallen in love have each thrown a bamboo ("zhu/trúc") leaf into the waters of a lake; if the two leaves float away together, the two young lovers will enjoy a life-long union. Their wish was granted so perfectly that the lake was called "Lake of the young girl's wish (Du fu tan 賭婦潭)".[3] On the other hand, if the word "mei (mai)" is written 梅, the two words "zhu mei (trúc mai) 竹梅" alludes to "The ballad of Changgan (*Changgan xing* 長干行)" by Li Bai 李白. In this case, it is the contraction of the expression "qing mei zhu ma 青梅竹馬 (green apricot and bamboo horse)", meaning the games of a young couple in love. However, the gloss that the majority of reliable commentators retain for the expression "trúc mai 竹枚 (dwarf bamboo and giant bamboo)" in the novel in verse *The Tale of Kiều* [Truyện Kiều 傳翹], by Nguyễn Du, is the friendship and first love between the two heroes, Kiều and Kim Trọng, a thwarted relationship between two young betrothed lovers separated by the vicissitudes of life. To stay faithful to this young love, Kiều is prepared to become an ox or a horse in a future life to pay his debt "爫身婁 馭填誼竹梅 Làm thân trâu ngựa đền nghì trúc mai (Even if I become an ox or a horse in a future life, I will pay you my debt with undying love)[4]". In this case, the popular symbolic prevails: the two sorts of bamboo, the small one ("trúc", word from the Chinese, meaning all bamboo in Vietnamese in preference to "tre") and the giant bamboo ("mai", *Dendrocalamus giganteus* Munro) are both considered remarkable for their regular internodes and for their straight trunks – qualities that reflect the scholarly symbolic.

Apart from the straightness of the trunk, the capacity of bamboo to return to its original position after being bent over by an external force – wind, pressure – shows its value for scholars, and beyond that, among ordinary people. As one of the most familiar plants to the Vietnamese, in their mind, it is naturally straight. On the other hand, a trunk that is unnaturally bent in natural surroundings hides a trap. And bamboo that is lying on a path indicates something suspect or even malevolent. Children are taught not to step over but to go round it because, as soon as one steps over or goes under it, the bamboo may suddenly become vertical (or distended). Indeed, bent bamboo (or a branch of bamboo) is often used to set snares and the detent force can be fearsome: most animals will approach without suspicion, but a person who has been carefully instructed since his tender years will be careful not to get too close.

Concerning funerals, in the south of Việt Nam, two expressions are used to describe the shape of a wooden coffin lid: if the cover is rectangular, it is called "cover in the shape of a square box (nắp tráp)", while, if it is domed, it is called "cover in the shape of a bamboo shoot sheath (nắp vỏ măng)".[5]

Bamboo and botanists

Since Linné (1707–1778), botanical classification has been based on the floral element of the plant. Botanists working on samples from herbariums note the differences in structure of the flowers through dissection and observation – if necessary, by using a microscope. Most botanical samples from expeditions by the plant collectors who have travelled the world for centuries almost all include an inflorescence. This is not always the case with bamboo because it flowers in an irregular manner: each flowering takes place after a gap of a variable number of years that can be up to a century or more. After flowering, bamboo dies – not only the clump of the particular variety but also all the examples of the same variety across continents – possibly due to the phenomenon of particular genetic memory. When one finds a bamboo specimen with flowers, it probably comes from a plant that no longer exists (see Figure 4.1). Phạm Hoàng Hộ, a well-known Vietnamese botanist who classified almost 100 species of bamboo, always notes when a specimen has irregular flowering: so *Bambusa variabilis* Munro ("tầm vông") has not flowered for a long time, *Bambusa bambos* (L.) Voss. ("tre gai rừng") has a flowering cycle of 50 years, *Dendrocalamus asper* (Schult.) Back. Ex Heyne ("tre mạnh tông") flowered once between 1967 to 1984.[6]

When bamboo does produce seeds, a more-or-less rare event according to the variety, forest people harvest it. It is eaten in the same way as rice. However, bamboo seed is only considered to be a supplement in times of food shortages. Vietnamese populations have noticed that bamboo flowers only very rarely and that the flowerings coincide with poor harvests. The bad omen of the flowering is followed by the production of seeds, which is considered as providential compensation.[7]

Figure 4.1 Flowering of a clump of bamboo, which then dies immediately, 2017. Available: https://vanhien.vn/news/tre-tro-hoa-51541 [Accessed: 15/06/2019].

Another common symbol has arisen from the particularity of the reproductive cycle of bamboo. Like all living beings, it reproduces sexually but its cycle is spread out over decades, even centuries, so that, in the common tongue, "bamboo in flower" ("tre nở hoa") is a bad omen because, after flowering, its death is necessarily imminent. All sexual reproduction is based on flowering, fruiting, then the germination and growth of the plant, with a clear distinction between the generations, whereas in the case of bamboo, one generation follows on to the next; the generations are simultaneous and mingled together. This is the meaning of the expression "tre già, măng mọc (tall bamboo ages, young bamboo shoot grows)".[8] In the same clump of bamboo, a young stalk emerges from the earth, not growing next to its parents but by its kin, as part of the existing clump that protects it. It is easy to understand that vegetative propagation (by cuttings or layering) has long been a favoured method of cultivation in Việt Nam. Another similar expression translates the natural order of life: "Tre già để chỗ cho măng ([it is normal that] old bamboo vacates its place for a young shoot)", and another pithy saying summarizes the paradox of an elderly person mourning the death of a young child: "Tre già khóc măng (Old bamboo weeps for young shoot)".

In a rice-based civilization cultivating almost exclusively a single gramineous crop, rice-growers have learned to be cautious of the invasive presence of that gramineous shrub – bamboo. This is why the farmers, while tending a bamboo

Bamboo as symbol 63

hedge around their dwellings as protection, will make sure that it stays at a safe distance from their house. "Bamboo bush (bụi tre)" has the connotation not only of a "distant" place but also somewhere to be "despised", considered to be "wild" rather than "inhabited". This is echoed in the popular saying that compares a plain earthenware jug thrown into a "bamboo thicket" with valued objects such as the "bronze bell or the lithophone": "Chuông khánh còn chẳng ăn ai, nữa là mảnh chĩnh vứt ngoài bụi tre (Bell of bronze or bell of stone are despised, so what is the value of a broken jug thrown into the bamboo thicket?)".[9] A comparison of this sort from the lips of a young girl is a subtle way of eliminating her rivals.

A characteristic of popular culture in Việt Nam should be noted here. It is never linear but proceeds comfortably in a dialectic manner: as soon as a quality is enounced or discovered, its opposite is immediately mentioned. In the word pair "tre, trúc" (bamboo and miniature bamboo), there is even a latent opposition. While the use of bamboo is widespread in all layers of society and the term "tle" (early form of "tre", bamboo) is known, as mentioned in Alexandre de Rhodes' *Dictionarium* and in Loureiro's *Flora*, this term appears extremely rarely in scholarly writings in Việt Nam, perhaps because, in the eyes of the elite, the term "nôm" is considered to be "coarse" ("Nôm na là cha mách qué", vernacular terms are a source of vulgarity).[10] Only the word "trúc" (miniature bamboo) is used to indicate not only miniature bamboo itself but also the whole bamboo family. "Tre" appears in a few cases such as "觜滝船似苺栁 Dưới sông thuyền tựa lá tre (On the river the boat is like a bamboo leaf/捄潮扎渃旗雺岂丕 Mái chèo rẽ nước, cờ che ngất trời (The oars slice the waves, the banners veil the immensity of the sky)" in the *Thiên Nam ngữ lục ngoại ký*[11]; "笠籟價黏苧初売 Lợp lều mái cỏ tranh xơ xác (Hut with a thatched roof in tatters)/[捄]技橋栁焠肯堯 Xỏ kẽ kèo tre đốt khẳng khiu (The gap between the bamboo beams, filled with your stump of a mortise)." In the *Xuân Hương thi tập*[12]; "払弘空冊別鞆 Chàng Hoàng không sách biết sao (Deprived of books, the young Hoàng has no other solution)/擾經廳学曰㕵脴箈 Mượn kinh mà học viết vào mảnh tre (than to borrow the Classics to study once he has copied them on strips of bamboo)" in the *Gia huấn*.[13] Similarly, in the *ca dao*, one finds "Chém tre, đẵn gỗ trên ngàn (Cut bamboo, fell trees in the forest)/Hữu thân, hữu khổ phàn nàn cùng ai (If there is suffering, no-one to whom to complain)".[14]

Nguyễn Trãi, the famous 15th-century scholar, is the only writer who used another name for bamboo "vầu" 笆, although this word is often used by villagers in documents describing practical uses of the plant.[15] This is even more evident in their use of bamboo plant names as a suffix. It is common knowledge that the Vietnamese often choose to use plant names as a suffix when naming a child, the plant representing the desired qualities for the children: for "trúc" (miniature bamboo), the term is combined with all the possible words for colours and all the imaginable virtues: "Bảo Trúc 寶竹 (precious bamboo)", "Băng Trúc 冰竹 (immaculate bamboo)", "Diễm Trúc 豔竹 (elegant bamboo)", "Hoàng Trúc 皇竹 (majestic bamboo)", "Ngọc Trúc 玉竹 (jade bamboo)", "Thanh Trúc 清竹 (brilliant bamboo)" but the word "tre" never appears in such a context! This anthroponymic phenomenon calls for two explanations: first of all, the attraction of an unusual and scholarly term "trúc" coupled happily with words representing noble materials or colours,[16]

64 *Bamboo: an anthropological and historical approach*

and above all because "tre" is the vernacular word for bamboo, definitely a useful plant but whose fate, compared to all other plants, can hardly be considered as enviable. It is felled, cut, cut up, split, bent and sawn up. After use, it is often thrown away, whether it was used as toothpick or became a blunted knife. Its only use is found in a few nicknames or pen names by people who wish to be part of the ordinary population and who dare to stand out in a servile society; this is the case in the pen names of Bút Tre ("Bamboo writing brush"), Tre Xanh ("Leafy green bamboo").

There is another paradox concerning bamboo: it grows in a compact mass and forms an impenetrable hedge, which is a quality. All over Asian countries that have been influenced by China, the symbol of a union that creates strength is often a bunch of bamboo sticks considered to be unbreakable, whereas a single branch could be broken. However, aesthetic considerations become important when the solitary state is eulogized. As the lyrics of the following two folk-songs suggest: "Trúc xinh, trúc mọc bờ ao/Em xinh, em đứng chỗ nào cũng xinh (A miniature bamboo is pretty if it grows at the edge of a pool/But you my sweetheart, you are pretty wherever you are)".[17] Variant: "Trúc xinh, trúc mọc đầu đình/Em xinh, em đứng một mình cũng xinh (Miniature bamboo is graceful if it grows by the communal house/But you are pretty and you need no other presence)".[18]

Bamboo fibre's properties of strength are also present in another folk-song comparing one's own belongings to those of someone else: "Của người bồ tát, của mình lạt buộc (One gives another person's belongings away as if one were Buddha, whereas one's own things are bound up tight with bamboo straps)". The sturdiness of bamboo strips easily becomes a synonym of avarice.

Vương Hồng Sển, one of the best specialists in Southern Việt Nam, tells a story that includes a fine symbol for bamboo. When offered money, through greediness, a person may be ready to sacrifice even the people who protect him and who are his benefactors. During the conquest of the six southern provinces by the French armies, bamboo hedges provided such impenetrable ramparts that, in order to get through them, the invaders used a clever stratagem: they threw silver and other valuable coins into the middle of the hedge. Under the cover of night, the soldiers inside who were protected by the hedge came out to cut down the hedge themselves in order to reach the treasure, opening the way to the enemy troops, who were no longer faced with an obstacle to their advance.[19]

This portrayal of bamboo illustrates the porous link between the culture of the scholar and that of the ordinary man. Also born and raised in the country, scholars remained close to the peasants. Even the emperor himself freely compared a brave defender of the marches to a "subject who acts as fence and barrier" for the country, using two types of bamboo protection ("bề tôi phên dậu"). The same expression is also used to indicate an area or a march that serves as the final rampart for the whole nation. A successful offensive is described as "thế dễ như chẻ tre (our situation is as favourable as that of someone splitting bamboo)", meaning easy penetration amongst enemy forces to overcome them.

The eminent scholar Nguyễn Trãi, mentioned earlier, not only enjoyed the company of the bamboo that graced his garden hedge, he was happy to live surrounded

Bamboo as symbol 65

by his simple bamboo furniture, symbols of a peaceful retirement. In the 16th century, Nguyễn Bỉnh Khiêm, another remarkable figure, also an adept of the secluded and quiet life, in several of his poems in "nôm", insisted on the use of bamboo shoots as nourishment, not only as a sign of frugality but also as representing an unworldly life in close contact with nature:

> With a spade, a hoe or a fishing rod,
> I potter, leaving others to their pleasures.
> Ingenuously, I choose the empty spaces;
> The better informed seek out noise and activity.
> In autumn I eat bamboo shoots, in winter I feed myself on pea sprouts.
> In the spring I bathe in the lotus lake, in summer, in my pond.
> Let us taste this wine sitting in the shade of an old tree.
> To be considered: are honours and riches anything but dreams?[20]
> ("Seclusion").

Nhàn

蔑埋蔑鉬蔑芹拘 Một mai, một cuốc, một cần câu
竦矨油埃醿趣芇 Thơ thẩn dù ai vui thú nào
些曳些尋尼永尾 Ta dại ta tìm nơi vắng vẻ,
趴坤趴典准唠哗 Người khôn người đến chốn lao xao.
秋咹芒竹冬咹稼 Thu ăn măng trúc, đông ăn giá.
春沁湖蓮复沁沟 Xuân tắm hồ sen, hạ tắm ao.
醴旦檜核些仕旺 Rượu đến cội cây ta sẽ uống,
忍祐富貴似占包 Nhìn xem phú quý tựa chiêm bao.

Nguyễn Bỉnh Khiêm.

Notes

1 *TT*, bản kỷ, q. VI, f ° 24a-24b.
2 Musée de la Monnaie de Paris, 1986, nᵒˢ V168, V259, V260; Thierry, François, 1988, nᵒ 1854a, 2002, nᵒˢ 441 et 521.
3 Liang Shaoren, juan VI in *Chinese Text Project* [Accessed: 05/04/2020].
4 Vers N°708. *Trans. auct*. See Nguyễn Văn Vĩnh, 1942, p. 182. The translation by Nguyễn Văn Vĩnh into French is, like the others, available on the site *Notes du Mont royal*. See the 1870 version of the text in vernacular writing in *The Vietnamese Nôm Preservation Foundation* [Accessed: 16/08/2021].
5 Vương Hồng Sển, 1993, p. 673.
6 Phạm Hoàng Hộ, 1993, vol. 6, pp. 753–4, 757, 762. See also later, p. 62, beliefs about this flowering.
7 Crévost, Lemarié, 1917, vol. 1, p. 88.
8 See *infra*, Chapter 6, p. 85–86.
9 *Tục ngữ phong dao*, vol. 2, 1957, p. 62. Nguyễn Lân, 1989, p. 61.
10 See Nguyễn Lân, *op. cit.*, p. 122.
11 Nguyễn Quang Hồng, 2015, vol. 2, p. 1919.
12 *Ibidem*.
13 Nguyễn Hữu Vinh et al., 2009, p. 1351.
14 *Tục ngữ phong dao*, vol. 2, p. 17.

66 *Bamboo: an anthropological and historical approach*

15 Trần Trọng Dương, 2014, p. 395.
16 Juxtaposition rules: scholarly words + adjectives of quality. No use of vernacular terms, except in rural parlance.
17 *Tục ngữ phong dao*, vol. 1, p. 311
18 *Ibidem*, p. 311. See also *Lý hạng ca dao*, f ° 40b.
19 Vương Hồng Sển, 1993, pp. 456–7.
20 *Trad. auct.* See Nguyễn Bỉnh Khiêm in Schneider, 1974, *BV* 79, p. 772.

5 Bamboo and power

While bamboo as plant and as material is present in all aspects of daily life,[1] it also plays an important role in the public domain. Numerous historical documents, such as the annals of the final reigns of the country, prove its importance in this area. In this chapter, the plant will be considered in all its aspects: cultivation, use and by-products. Its polyvalence demonstrates its special place in imperial ritual, public celebrations, in the workings of state bureaucracy, weaponry and defence. Texts in classical Chinese with full translations are presented in this chapter to demonstrate as far as possible the multiple facets and all the complexities of the plant. This close scrutiny of bamboo reveals the wide range of its uses as a plant and as a material. These official writings should be interpreted as recognition of the important role this modest plant plays in multiple domains.

1) Bamboo at the centre of imperial ritual and public celebration

Bamboo played an important role in imperial religious ritual. Two sorts of ritual hedges had their own specific regulations; for example, around the mounds raised for the ceremonies for the Earth ("Xã" 社) and for the Harvest ("Tắc" 稷): "the lower esplanade is square and each side measures 66,76 m.[2] It is bordered with bamboo, with fine quality trees on the inside ("lương" 良)".[3] In the same way, around the area for ploughing the first furrow, "this space is surrounded by a bamboo hedge".[4] For ritual purposes, the bamboo basket-work utensils were subject to strict specifications; for example, for the making the ritual accessories used during Imperial commemoration ceremonies: "The 'biên' 籩 is a bowl woven from bamboo and is used to hold fruit during a religious ceremony. It has a brass lining (so that it holds water)".[5] The rules stipulate the name used for the object, how to describe its use, the shape and/or colour. There are variants of this type of container: "woven bamboo baskets, round with feet and a lid ('phỉ' 篚), reinforced inside with a lining of wooden slats, painted yellow all over"[6]; whereas a "khuông" 筐 is a square container in woven bamboo, a "phi" 篚 [is a] "basket in woven bamboo, round in shape, to carry flowers and fruit for worship".[7]

DOI: 10.4324/9781003350347-7

68   *Bamboo: an anthropological and historical approach*

Bamboo also played an important part in public celebrations. The use of fireworks made of bamboo was allowed in the 19th century by imperial decree:

> On the thirtieth day (the eve of Tết) and during the three first days of the first moon, custom requires that after the ceremonies in the temples and at Phụng Tiên palace, firecrackers made of bamboo tube or paper should be set off ("phát đồng thanh chỉ pháo" 發筒聲紙砲). In the olden days our ancestors set off bamboo tubes ("bạo trúc" 爆竹) to rid the country of pestilence ("lệ khí" 癘氣) and to welcome the spring".[8]

The same remark was made in 14th century by Lê Trắc who, in his *Abbreviated Records of An Nam*, uses the same term "bạo trúc" 爆竹 (bamboo that explodes): "That night (the thirtieth day, the eve of Tết), [. . .] the population open their doors to light firecrackers made with bamboo tubes.[9]" In the 19th century, bamboo is preferred, as it is considered to be less dangerous than metal devices as illustrated by this 1837 text:

> The population are forbidden to use metal tubes for firecrackers ("phóng thiết đồng" 放鐵筒). From then onwards in Huế city and in the towns in the surrounding provinces, mandarin officials, soldiers and the population are allowed to use firecrackers made of bamboo tubes ("bạo trúc" 爆竹), or made with paper ("chỉ pháo" 紙砲), during various celebrations, but on no account are they permitted to use metal tubes.[10]

To celebrate the emperor's birthday, it was customary to erect fake mountains ("giả sơn" 假山) built on a bamboo frame. Over a period of nearly 50 years, the *Complete Book of the Historical Records of Đại Việt* provide a wealth of detail demonstrating that this commemorative event became a national institution. Introduced in the year Ất Dậu (985), in year six of the Thiên Phúc era (in the reign of Đại Hành of the Early Lê), this tradition was carried on into the following century: "In autumn, at the full moon of the seventh month on the Emperor's birthday, orders were given to build scaffolding on a vessel, midway across the river, to imitate mountains, to be called 'Southern Peaks'". Then festivities with boat races, which later became customary, were organized.[11] Later on, in the Bính Ngọ year (1006), in year 13 of the Ứng Thiên era (of the reign Ngọa Triều of the Early Lê), the emperor's birthday was celebrated in a similar manner in winter at the tenth moon and was followed by a banquet for the mandarin officials.[12] But in 1021, year 12 of the Thuận Thiên era (in the reign of Thái Tổ of the Lý), the sovereign's birthday was in springtime.

> On this occasion scenery named "Southern Peak to wish ten thousand years" of longevity to the Emperor was built around bamboo frameworks. On the mountaintop, erected in front of the Gate of Supreme Bliss, moving figures of birds and animals were installed, all with a multitude of strange and novel features. The Emperor also ordered a chorus of imitations of the animals' calls to amuse the guests at the court banquet.[13]

Bamboo and power 69

Beginning as a single commemorative installation, this festival developed into a permanent institution, and the fake mountain on its bamboo framework became a complicated and costly automaton. The following year, the same emperor "having noticed that the construction ritual of the fake mountain in bamboo for the festival of Celestial Fulfilment exhausted the population, abolished the ritual, only maintaining the banquet".[14] This measure benefitting the people lasted for six years: "At the sixth moon (of year one of the Thiên Thành era (1028) in the reign of Thái Tông of the Lý), the birthday of the Emperor was chosen to celebrate the festival of Celestial Fulfilment. On the Dragon Esplanade, bamboo was used to construct 'Southern Peaks (to wish) ten thousand years', modelled on a five-peak mountain".[15] The construction needed to be grandiose enough to provide space for musicians to perform from it, so that the automatons performed to a musical accompaniment.

> In the middle of the central peak, rose the Mountain of Longevity, and the other four peaks represented the White Crane Mountains. On these hills, figures of flying birds and other moving animals were placed, and half way up the slopes were dragon genies, and all this among various banners decorated with gold and jade. Musicians were ordered to play flutes and trumpets inside the grottoes, and singing and dancing was performed for the pleasure of all the guests at a banquet for the mandarin officials. Henceforth regulations were put in place concerning the five-peak mountains.[16]

Important political events also provided an opportunity for the sovereigns to demonstrate their largesse. Fans made of mottled bamboo ("ban" 斑) were distributed as gifts by the emperor to reward his deserving subjects. Sometimes, these rewards were given to the victorious army, along with "fabrics of fine and raw silks ("sa" 紗, "trừu" 紬), as well as handkerchiefs ("thủ phách" 手帕)",[17] and they were also given to scholars or military officials from the fourth rank, along with "red taffetas for turbans ".[18] The variety of bamboo mentioned earlier, which was highly valued, was also used for other articles such as those mentioned in *The Descriptive Geography of the Emperor Đồng Khánh* in the sub-prefecture Thụy Nguyên in Thanh Hóa: "In the canton of Ngọc Lặc a variety of mottled bamboo ('ban trúc' 斑竹) grows and it can be used for making palanquins ('võng cống' 輞樻)".[19] This type of "võng cống" is quite rare but I (Đ.T.H.) photographed one in 1982 called "võng tre" by the population in Đào Xá (see Figure 5.1–2).

2) Bamboo as central to the functioning of Imperial bureaucracy

2a) Bamboo and taxation

This issue is a complex one. To simplify the study of the regulations, firstly, the taxation concerning bamboo plantation will be studied, then that concerning byproducts of bamboo, and finally, the use of bamboo screens. As noted earlier, the planting of bamboo can be a remunerative activity; taxation of the land used for

70 *Bamboo: an anthropological and historical approach*

Figure 5.1–2 1. Palanquin made of bamboo strips "võng tre". 2. Detail. Đào Xá Village. Phú Thọ Province. 1982. Photograph by Đinh Trọng Hiếu.

this purpose was substantial, as illustrated by this 1840 provision: "the fiscal provision from the Bố Chính prefecture concerning elephant grass and bamboo: 30 cash ('văn' 文) less than elsewhere. This will serve as an example for taxation in other constituencies".[20] It is curious to see that coconut plantations and bamboo groves are both taxed at the same level. "New taxes on the agricultural lands in

Bamboo and power 71

the South: land planted with bamboo and rice-fields given over to coconut are in the third category"[21]. Even certain by-products of bamboo such as planks and slats were taxed, as shown in this 1827 provision: "Henceforth these dues will be transferred to the Treasury as the administration has received compensation concerning this public utility spending"[22]. These dues were so onerous that, in the end, they were abolished and in 1853 the taxation of bamboo and stakes was discontinued.[23]

As taxes were often paid in the form of paddy rice, the bamboo basket-ware used as containers also contributed to the payment of these dues, as noted by Lê Quý Đôn in the 18th century:

> Granaries for rice and paddy come in the form of thick racks in woven bamboo that are bent round into cylinder form. These basket-ware racks are almost 8 meters long and 7 meters high, to be provided by those who have rice fields. A village that has 1000 measures ("thưng")[24] of paddy must provide 5 of these basket-ware racks and, if a payment in money is preferred, the payment is equivalent, in this case, to 120 cash. This money, which can be paid at the tax office, will be used to pay the collectors employed by the office ("cai lại") and the mandarin officials ("cai trưng"). Thus, a sub-prefecture must deliver 100 of these racks; the payment for the employee to guard the granary, as well as the soldiers present for this task, is estimated as more than 10 of these. Also gifts must be delivered to the "four pillars" of the Court, to the six ministries, to the mandarin officials in the administrative and fiscal offices, at a rate of 20 racks for each mandarin official by sub prefecture; the remainder will be handed to the Treasury.[25]

The charges for these basket-ware racks are then listed "for the different sub-prefectures in the provinces of Thuận Hóa and of Quảng Nam for the Kỷ Sửu year. The prefecture of Diên Khánh, its three sub-prefectures, the district of Bình Khang, its two prefectures, the prefecture of Bình Thuận, its two sub-prefectures, the prefecture of Gia Định, its three sub-prefectures and its mountain district ("châu"), do not have this custom of payment in the form of bamboo basket-ware"[26].

The relevance of this paragraph is not so much the tax itself but the manner in which it was set by "quarter of a rack (góc cót)" as described here:

> There is a customary practice at the Treasury: for 1 000 measures[27] of paddy, carrying cost 5 dimes ("tiền"). There is this type of taxation payable in bamboo basket-ware, at a rate of 4 items of basket-ware for 1000 measures of paddy rice. Each basket-ware rack is sub-divided into "corners (góc cót)", one of these corners will be paid to the Treasury, and that payment will be 2 dimes, monies may be used instead of basket-ware for 3 items, one item being worth 2 dimes. 62 and a half measures are contained in one quarter of a rack, in monies that is equivalent to 30 cash ("đồng"); 31 measures and 2 half measures ("cáp") are contained in half of a quarter rack, worth in monies 35 cash.[28]

72 *Bamboo: an anthropological and historical approach*

Also included for taxation were desirable items in bamboo intended as "tribute" to the emperor. For everyday use, matting was made of rushes, but only the finest and most durable bamboo matting could be included in the offerings to the Sovereign as "annual tribute":

At the eleventh moon, Kế Bà Tử was acknowledged (by Nguyễn Phúc Chu, r.1691–1725) as prince of the Thuận Thành marches. He must take care of the people and the men at arms and pay the annual tribute in the form of: 2 male elephants, 20 yellow bulls, 6 elephant tusks, 10 rhinoceros horns, 500 lengths of white cloth, 50 kilos of beeswax, 200 fish skins, 400 baskets of "phí sa" 沸沙 ("boiling sand": in contact with water this sand starts to boil as it contains caustic soda. It is then used as shampoo), 500 white mats in woven bamboo ("bạch điệm" 白簟), 200 ebony trunks, 1 long boat. As for items previously confiscated, such as seals, swords, saddles, horses and captives, all will be returned and discharged.[29]

2b) The role of bamboo in the control framework of Imperial bureaucracy

Bamboo identification tablets were commonly used in situations concerning recognition, introductions and giving testimony. Here are some regulations: in 1796, there was to be distribution of "authentication tablets in bamboo ("hợp phù" 合符)"[30] to soldiers and artisans employed in public works to prevent misdemeanours such as theft by imposter soldiers, tax evasion or failure to report for statute labour by village fugitives. From then on, they were obliged to wear an identification tablet on their belt for authentication. In order to prevent fraud and identity theft, from 1832 onwards, public servants were obliged show a "cylindrical bamboo (or wooden) document case engraved with the indication of the bureau concerned, and an order number. This document case is to be used in the case of a prefecture, it being forbidden to use a similar document case from another prefecture".[31] In contrast, with bamboo being convenient for concealing things, it could be used for nefarious purposes, as shown by this example from 1839: "taking advantage of the craze for opium, smugglers hide their products in bamboo tubes where it is difficult to detect"[32].

State bureaucracy in Việt Nam being based on the circulation of written documents, it may not even be necessary to remind some readers of the importance of the Imperial postal system ("trạm" 站) and the place of bamboo in this institution. Remarks concerning the sealed documents carried are included in a regulation dating from 1859.

Concerning sealed secret documents and those concerning military matters, two strong, well-dried bamboo tubes are required, one larger than the other. The documents in question must be placed in two closed and sealed envelopes, then placed in the small bamboo tube, to be closed at the other end of the internode using glued paper, this is repeated two or three times, stamping each seal. These papers must be attached with string, and then stamped again.

Bamboo and power 73

Figure 5.3 A rider carrying the Imperial post. *Le Tour du Monde*, 1880, p. 313. Wood engraving.

The small tube is placed inside the big tube, to be closed in the same way (glued paper covers to be stamped and sealed, then tied in place with string).[33]

Such official documents were entrusted to either runners ("lính trạm" or "phu trạm") or riders on horseback ("mã thượng").
An observer in the late 19th century, Dutreil de Rhins, reported:

these couriers do not wear a special uniform and I have rarely seen one armed with a gun. They wear a strap over their shoulder to carry the bamboo tube containing the dispatches, and seem to be welded to their small horses whose normal pace is a very rapid trot. The bells on the collar of their horse announce their arrival from afar. The road, especially in the villages is immediately cleared of anything that might delay the royal messenger; the boatmen hold the ferries ready at river crossings and ahead of the 'trạm', a fresh courier will be waiting to take over the relay at the same speed.[34]

The same word, "trạm", was used to indicate both the rapid delivery of official correspondence and also the transport for mandarin officials, their luggage and state supplies as well as the locations for the relay. This latter is in fact the first meaning of the term.

This hut, comprised of one single room, is what is called a "trạm" (an abbreviation of "dịch trạm" 驛站), a place where the traveller can find shelter and

74 *Bamboo: an anthropological and historical approach*

where the government always has couriers at its service. The "trạm" are set up at intervals along the main road across Annam, the route being established as the conquest progresses through each province. The initial organisation of the "trạm" and the Annam postal service dates from the eleventh century, when this country (the Central area, or Annam) was still part of the Champa kingdom.[35]

2c) Bamboo in public infrastructure

Imperial granaries for paddy rice were carefully managed and bamboo was a major component in the construction of these buildings. For example, "bamboo tubes were installed to ventilate public granaries[36] to prevent mould appearing in the paddy".[37] Bamboo was also used for fire prevention in these buildings, as shown in an imperial edict in 1839: "to a governor who requested a tiled roof for these places the Emperor replied suggesting that bamboo racks should be rendered and placed over the thatch roofs to avoid the risk of fire".[38] Another paragraph in the *Veritable Records of the Great South* reported:

> The Emperor inspects the reserves in the capital. He remarks that the soldiers stationed to guard these places spread large bamboos ("mao trúc" 茅竹)[39] and requests that they be reprimanded. Henceforth, in places close to the reserves (Office of the Imperial House, Arsenal, Personal Treasure of the Emperor), the Capital Granary, near to warehouses for powder, saltpetre ("diêm tiêu" 鹽硝) it will be forbidden to place inflammable goods such as large bamboo, coconut foliage or dry fuel. Those who disobey will be given serious punishments. If there is a fire they will be decapitated and their head displayed to the public.[40]

Unlike the employment of bamboo in the military that was soon superseded, it remained in use for protecting dykes. Hydraulic works were frequently carried out during the Nguyễn dynasty (1802–1945). An extract from the regulations of the Dyke Administration Bureau in the mid-19th century is an example of the use of bamboo in this domain:

> For the maintenance of the dykes, the customary regulations for planting bamboo must be observed. Where bamboo has not yet been planted, this must be done to protect the dykes from waves and wind, and thus the necessary bamboo is available when required. Large baskets (in bamboo) must be kept in stock, filled with earth, and also bamboo and wood.[41]

If dykes threaten to collapse, bamboo trunks are the chosen material for strengthening them. In 1837, the emperor "ordered repayment to the population for supplying wood and bamboo for making stakes ("chang" 椿) and fences ("sách" 柵) and should be made on the basis of a high price".[42] Bamboo is not only used in building dams and/or for strengthening dykes, but also for making large open-weave baskets ("trúc lâu" 竹簍), which, when filled with earth or rocks, provide excellent obstruction formwork, similar to the formwork for concrete used nowadays. In 1858, this method was used to "drain a channel, in order to prevent French sampans from entering from Đại Chiêm Bay".[43] However, before the rainy season, it was necessary to plan for stocks of earth, bamboo and wood. Quoting a Chinese saying, Emperor Minh Mạng said, "a (single) missing basket (filled with earth) destroys all the efforts made to build a mountain": "一簣虧山 Nhất quy khuy sơn".[44]

Given later are the measurements of the dykes for the planning of these works and, as importantly, the materials needed, as stipulated in Article 4 "estimation of costs" in the regulations of the Northern Dykes Administration Office:

> Upstream on the Red River, and in its middle section, the dykes are 8m wide at the top, the base is 28m wide and 4.80m high. For 4m of dyke, plan for 54 piles of earth on a flat surface; downstream, the dyke is 6m wide at the top, the base is 20m wide, and 4m high. For 4m of dyke, plan for 32 heaps of earth 2m high. For medium waterways, the width at the top of the dyke is 4,80m, the base is 16m wide, the height is 4m. For 4m of dyke, plan for 26 heaps of earth. For small streams, width at the top is 3,6m, the base is 12m wide, the height is 3,6m; for 4m of dyke, plan for 17 heaps of earth 2,20m high. Where there is muddy ground for a depth of between 0,4m to 1,6m, for 4m of dyke, plan for 73 wooden piles and 6 green bamboos ("thanh trúc" 青竹). If the mud is at least 2 to 2,4m deep, for 4m of dyke, plan for 73 lengths of timber and 6 green bamboos. A budget must be planned for buying materials to construct dykes: framework ("cốt" 骨), piles ("chang tử" 椿子), props ("hàn" 翰), supports ("dực" 翼), long pontoons, crossbeam pontoons, as well as, on both sides (of the dyke) wooden gutters ("mộc cừ" 木渠) and wooden crossbeams ("mộc cương" 木橺).[45]

Here is an extract from Article 7 "Protection (of dykes)" from the regulations of the Northern Dykes Administration Office: "At the base of the dykes damming the big rivers, bamboo must be planted every 24m, with 6 plants ('chu' 株) for every 4 m of dyke, in order to protect these constructions from flood water flow ('cuồng lan' 狂瀾), and also so that if it is necessary to rebuild the dyke, material will be to hand. But it is forbidden to cut down this bamboo for any other purpose".[46]

The use of the bamboo hedge in civil society, variable according to location, is explained in a passage in the *Veritable Records of the Great South*. This describes building a temporary town in 1833 at Châu Đốc, by setting up barriers of felled bamboo on all four sides, enclosing a granary, a public building, which could also be used as a residence.[47] In the Highlands or near the borders, the situation was different from the Delta area as expressed in this regulation, dating from 1871: "In order to protect animals, they must be gathered together in enclosures surrounded by mounds of earth and/or planted with prickly bamboo".[48] As for Hà Tiên "its situation as an island means that there is a shortage of building land and public buildings are also used as dwellings; barracks and jails are surrounded by a hedge ('ly' 籬) which proves to be insufficient for protection when the enemy fires on it

76 Bamboo: an anthropological and historical approach

from their boats".[49] Finally installations in bamboo basketwork were sometimes suggested using "thick racks of bamboo for use as a barrier".[50]

3) Military uses of bamboo

Although bamboo hedges – a category that includes stakes planted in earth banks – surrounded civilian areas and sites with a ritual connotation as mentioned earlier, their purpose was mainly military and also satisfied various needs.

The use of bamboo, thorny or not, to make a hedge around fortifications was an early practice. There are several passages in *Complete Book of the Historical Records of Đại Việt* and in the *Veritable Records of the Great South* that mention this use:

> In the Kỷ Mão year (1399), the second year of the Kiến Tân era [. . .], Trần Ninh was ordered to command men from the prefecture of Thanh Hóa to plant thorny bamboo around the citadel, in the south from Đốn Sơn, in the north from An Tôn up to the Bào Đàm gate, in the west from Khả Lăng market to Vực Sơn up to the Lỗi Giang river. All this created an external rampart around the citadel. Anyone who stole the bamboo shoots would be given the death penalty.[51]

For surrounding the enemy, in 1834, the emperor considered that "outside (a surrounded citadel), along the earth banks, it is necessary to secretly install bamboo stakes, place iron rods ("lộc giác" 鹿角) as well as caltrops ("tật lê" 蒺藜)".[52] However, as the sovereign remarked, "when surrounded, the enemy has a tendency to come out and flee, and to prevent them doing so, the surrounding army must build progressively higher and wider levees, with, on the outside, bamboo stakes and wooden horses ("mộc mã" 木馬)".[53]

For protecting the gunners, in 1833, a recommendation suggested: "on either side of a gun emplacement, levees should be built using large woven bamboo racks. These will take the form of large cylinders filled with earth to be used as bunkers for the gunners. Then they will not worry about return fire from the enemy, and be confident in aiming at and hitting their targets".[54]

To consolidate defences and undermine the enemy's, particularly for encircling a citadel such as Gia Định, in 1832, orders were issued

> to 2000 civilian auxiliaries to make a good number of large open weave bamboo baskets ("sọt"/orig. ms. "lâu" 簍) to fill them with earth and stones and to bring them at night to a place near the ramparts and, with the assistance of the soldiers, to finish consolidating the defences at these locations. During undermining for military purposes, if the army requires bamboo or wood, or various other materials, these can be taken from the inhabitants, but it must be explained that unfortunately these are temporary measures and that compensation will be distributed when the situation allows.[55]

For the hedges surrounding special guard posts ("đồn bảo" 屯堡), "plantations of bamboo and trees"[56] or "earth fortifications planted with thorny bamboo"[57] were

Bamboo and power 77

required. These examples show the extensive use of bamboo for military purposes. In a regulation dating from 1862, the method to be used for crossing ditches planted with bamboo stakes was set out in these terms: "by casting bamboo gangways covered with planks over the ditches, it is possible to pursue the enemy speedily and inflict severe losses".[58] The enemy could, of course, use the same strategy to invade a stronghold.

Passive obstruction created by placing obstacles on a riverbed to prevent the movement of groups of bandits was widely recommended in the latter part of the 19th century, either by barring waterways with "bamboo rafts attached to metal chains across the river"[59] or by immersing huge bamboo sacks filled with stones and lumps of earth.[60] A similar method was also used, but on land: "large square baskets of woven bamboo ('trúc khuông' 竹筐) are filled with earth and used to consolidate breaches in the ramparts".[61]

Bamboo by-products such as frameworks made of slats or racks were used during wartime, as described in the following strategy put in place to frighten the enemy.

In the year Ất Dậu (1285), year seven of the Thiệu Bảo era (in the reign of Nhân Tông) of the Trần dynasty [. . .], while the enemy was surrounding Phù Ninh prefecture, in its defence, prefect Hà Đặc strengthened his positions on mount Trĩ Sơn. Hà Đặc ordered bamboo frameworks to be made to imitate large human silhouettes. These were dressed and taken out at dusk. Enormous arrows were also planted in wooden planks to make the enemy believe that they [the Đại Việt] had weapons that could penetrate great thicknesses. The enemy forces were scared to the point of not daring to engage in combat.[62]

Similarly, in 1840 bamboo racks were used by the military as a decoy target for a gunship: "a raft is built in the shape of a ship with a mock sail made of a bamboo rack, to be used as a training target in gunship firing practice".[63]

Bamboo was also used to make many different weapons. An 1829 regulation provides an important technical detail: "For a weapon and/or the handle of a weapon trunks of solid bamboo ("thực" 湜) are used".[64] The word "thực", better known with the general meaning of "true", requires an explanation. Here, it has the specific meaning of "full, solid" and indicates bamboo whose medullary cavity is very narrow, making it very strong. A common variety of bamboo in Việt Nam, "tầm vông" (*Bambusa variabilis*), is particularly popular for crafting weapons. It is the same for "piaozhu" 篻竹 mentioned by Dai Kaizhi [Jin dynasty, 266–420] in his *Treatise on Bamboo* quoted by Lê Quý Đôn: "With 'jinzhu 筋竹' spears are made that are sought all over the four seas, those that grow in Rinan (Nhật Nam) bear the special name 'piaozhu' (phiếu trúc 篻竹). Jinzhu are two 'zhang' long and several 'cun' in diameter".[65]

In the late 19th century, bamboo was still being used "to make spears ('sáo' 槊) and staffs as defensive weapons".[66] It was also a forerunner of the flame-thrower, as described in the 1809 order addressed to (the Province of) Bình Định for the yearly supply of 3,000 "bamboo tubes that breath fire ('hỏa phôn trúc đồng' 火噴竹筒)".[67] Bamboo was also used to construct shields, as shown in a text dated

78 Bamboo: an anthropological and historical approach

1780: "Navy shipbuilders use the wood of Hopea (long stemmed *Dipterocar-paceae)*[68] to make boats with long rudders, where the deck is shielded with thick bamboo racks intended to protect the rowers while the foot soldiers are ready to engage in combat".[69] And also, as reported by Lê Quý Đôn, when bamboo was still only at the shoot stage (in the southern regions of the Chinese Empire), it was used to make strings for cross-bows.[70]

Notes

1 See *infra*, Part Two.
2 21 "trượng" and 6 "thước" in the original ms. Measurements, expressed in "trượng" and in "thước" in the original text, have been converted into meters for easier reading, with 1 "trượng" equivalent to roughly 4 m. and 1 "thước" equalling 0,46m.
3 *TL*, *cb*, kỷ II, q. LXXXII, f ° 15b. Minh Mệnh 13 [1832], 7th moon.
4 *TL*, *cb*, kỷ II, q. LXXVIII, f ° 19a. Minh Mệnh 13 [1832], 1st moon.
5 *TL*, *cb*, kỷ II, q. LVIII, f ° 6a-b. Minh Mệnh 10 [1829], 3rd moon.
6 *TL*, *cb*, kỷ II, q. CLXXI, f ° 5b. Minh Mệnh 17 [1836], 7th moon.
7 *TL*, *cb*, kỷ III, q. XIV, f ° 10a, Thiệu Trị 1 [1841], 12th moon.
8 *TL*, *cb*, kỷ II, q. LXXVII, f ° 13b. Minh Mệnh 12 [1831], 11th moon.
9 Lê Trắc, q. 1, f ° 17b.
10 *TL*, *cb*, kỷ II, q. CLXXVII, f ° 19b. Minh Mệnh 18 [1837], 1st moon.
11 *TT*, bản kỷ, q. I, f ° 17a.
12 *TT*, bản kỷ, q. I, f ° 27a.
13 *TT*, bản kỷ, q. II, f ° 9a.
14 *Ibidem*.
15 *TT*, bản kỷ, q. II, f ° 16b-17a.
16 *Ibidem*.
17 *TL*, *cb*, kỷ II, q. XXXIX, f ° 16a. Minh Mệnh 7 [1826], 6th moon.
18 *TL*, *cb*, kỷ II, q. XXVII, f ° 19a. Minh Mệnh 5 [1824], 5th moon.
19 "Võng cổng", word for word: palanquin suspended from a thick wooden pole. *ĐKĐDC.*, vol. 2, f ° 58a, p. 1182.
20 *TL*, *cb*, kỷ II, q. CCIX, f ° 10a, Minh Mệnh 21 [1840], 1st moon.
21 *TL*, *cb*, kỷ II, q. CLXXII, f ° 10b. Minh Mệnh 17 [1836], 8th moon.
22 *TL*, *cb*, kỷ II, q. XLIX, f ° 8a. Minh Mệnh 8 [1827], 11th moon.
23 *TL*, *cb*, kỷ IV, q. IX, f ° 9a. Tự Đức 6 [1853], 2nd moon.
24 Or nearly 3 000 litres.
25 *PBTL*, [1977], p. 142.
26 *Ibidem*, p. 144.
27 Or almost 3 000 litres.
28 *PBTL*, [1977], pp. 164–5.
29 *TL*, tb, q. 7, f ° 9b-10a [1694], 11th moon. On the role of Po Saktiraydaputih (Kế Bà Tử), key figure in the history of the Campa who became king of Bal Pandurang, cf. Weber, 2005, vol. 1, pp. 53–4.
30 "Hợp phù" 合符: a bamboo tablet divided lengthwise and used as testimony. Each of the interested parties retained one half. The matching of the two halves when put back together was proof of authenticity. *TL*, *cb*, kỷ II, q. VIII, f ° 16a-b [1796], 3rd moon.
31 *TL*, *cb*, kỷ II, q. LXXXI, f ° 5a-b. Minh Mệnh 13 [1832], 9th moon.
32 *TL*, *cb*, kỷ II, q. CCI, f ° 10b. Minh Mệnh 20 (1839), 4th moon.
33 *TL*, *cb*, kỷ IV, q.XXI, f ° 5b. Tự Đức 12 [1859], 7th moon.
34 Dutreuil de Rhins, 1889, p. 169.
35 *Ibidem*, p. 154.

36 Bamboo was also used to carry water. The *Veritable Records of the Great South* mention a piped system supplying the imperial city for watering the gardens *TL*, *cb*, kỷ VI, q.IX, f° 36b. Đồng Khánh 3 [1888], 3rd moon.
37 *TL*, *cb*, kỷ I, q.XXXIX, f° 4b-5a. Gia Long 8 [1809], 8th moon.
38 *TL*, *cb*, kỷ II, q.CCIV, f° 6a. Minh Mệnh 20 [1839], 7th moon.
39 Máo zhú/mao trúc" 茅竹 equivalent to "mao zhu/mao trúc" 毛竹. Although the Ricci dictionary of plants gives a scientific equivalent for "mao zhu/mao trúc" including the species and the names of authors, this is an extrapolation. *Phyllostachys pubescens* Mazel ex H. de Lehaie [= *Phyllostachys heterocycla* Mift.] Moso (Japanese) – Large bamboo (11–25m) from the Yangzi basin and further south. Introduced in Japan and then in Europe and in America as an ornamental. Much cultivated in southern China. Introduced in northern China. The most widespread bamboo in China: construction, furniture, tools, objects, paper. Shoots much appreciated, also used for medicine under the name of "mao sun" 毛筍 (member of the grasses genus).
40 *TL*, *cb*, kỷ II, q. L., f° 19b-20a Minh Mệnh 9 [1828], 2nd moon.
41 *TL*, *cb*, kỷ II, q.LIV, f° 16a. Minh Mệnh 9 [1828], 9th moon. On hydraulics, see Poisson, 2009.
42 *TL*, *cb*, kỷ II, q.CLXXXII, f° 26b. Minh Mệnh 18 [1837], 6th moon.
43 *TL*, *cb*, kỷ IV, q.XIX, f° 17b. Tự Đức 11 [1858], 8th moon.
44 *TL*, *cb*, kỷ II, q. LXVI, f° 11b. Minh Mệnh 11 [1830], 4th leap moon.
45 *TL*, *cb*, kỷ I, q. XXXIX, f° 9a-b. Gia Long 8 [1809], 9th moon.
46 *TL*, *cb*, kỷ I, q. XXXIX, f° 10a. Gia Long 8 [1809], 9th moon.
47 *TL*, *cb*, kỷ II, q. XCV, f° 11b, Minh Mệnh 14 [1833], 5th moon.
48 *TL*, *cb*, kỷ IV, q. XLV, f° 14a. Tự Đức 21 [1871], 9th moon.
49 *TL*, *cb*, kỷ IV, q. XVII, f° 41a. Tự Đức 10 [1857], 12th moon.
50 *TL*, *cb*, kỷ II, q. XLIV, f° 7b. Minh Mệnh 8 [1827], 3rd moon.
51 *TT*, bản kỷ, q. VIII, f° 36a.
52 *TL*, *cb*, kỷ II, q. CXXIX, 9b. Minh Mệnh 15 [1834], 6th moon. "Lộc giác": trunks with branches sharpened to a point used as obstacles in the form of deer antlers.
53 *TL*, *cb*, kỷ II, q. CX, f° 9b. Minh Mệnh 14 [1833], 10th moon. "Mộc mã": abbreviation of "mộc mã tử" 木馬子 was a military defensive structure shaped like a pommel horse.
54 *TL*, *cb*, kỷ II, q. CVIII. f° 9b. Minh Mệnh 14 [1833], 10th moon.
55 *TL*, *cb*, kỷ II, q. CXII, f° 14b. Minh Mệnh 14 [1833], 11th moon.
56 *TL*, *cb*, kỷ II, q. LXXXIV, f° 5a. Minh Mệnh 13 [1832], 9th leap moon.
57 *TL*, *cb*, kỷ IV, q. LXI, f° 49b. Tự Đức 32 [1879], 6th moon.
58 *TL*, *cb*, kỷ IV, q. XXVII, f° 16a. Tự Đức 15 [1862], 8th leap moon.
59 *TL*, *cb*, kỷ IV, q. XXXVIII, f° 28a. Tự Đức 21 [1868], 4th leap moon.
60 These measures were recommended by Trần Tiễn Thành. Cf. Đào Duy Anh, 1944, p. 107.
61 *TL, tb,* q.V, f° 14b, [1672], 11th moon.
62 *TT*, bản kỷ, q. V, f° 49a
63 *TL*, *cb*, kỷ II, q. CCXVIII, f° 28b-29a. Minh Mệnh 21 [1840], 10th moon.
64 *TL*, *cb*, kỷ II, q. LXI, f° 33b. Minh Mệnh 10 [1829], 9th moon.
65 *VĐLN*, q.IX, f° 72b. Dai Kaizhi, *Zhupu* 竹譜, ed. Waseda, ms. 14–00807, f°s 6a-b. *VĐLN*, q.IX, f° 72a. This bamboo measured 4,8 m, as a *zhang* 丈 contained seven feet *chi* 尺 and that the foot in the Western Jin period was 24cm (National Bureau of Measurement, China History Museum and Palace Museum, 1984, pp. 16–17). *Jin* 筋 means "tendon", "resistant".
66 *TL*, *cb*, kỷ VI, q. IV, f°24a. Đồng Khánh 1 [1886], 6th moon.
67 *TL*, *cb*, kỷ I, q. XXXVII, f°6a. Gia Long 8 [1809], 1st moon.
68 Lê Quý Đôn has written a lengthy description of this tree. *PBTL*, [1977], p. 319.
69 *TL*, *cb*, kỷ I, q. I, f°11a [1780], 7th moon. [Two identical entries.]
70 *VĐLN*, q.IX, f °72b.

Part 2

Bamboo iconography

This part will be based on two major sources, the *Mechanics and Crafts of the People of Annam* and the *Gia Định Art School monography*. The first three chapters, built on the first one, will deal with bamboo in northern Việt Nam. The last chapter, built on the second, will focus on bamboo in southern Việt Nam.

The drawings copied from wood engravings made by local craftsmen – Nguyễn Văn Đang (1874–1956), Nguyễn Văn Giai, Phạm Văn Tiêu et Phạm Trọng Hải[1]– from a printed collection edited by Henri Oger provide a wealth of information concerning Vietnamese material culture. For many years, this collection was only available for consultation in only a few libraries but is now available for research purposes in an edition published in 2009 (on CD and on paper) by Olivier Tessier and Philippe Le Failler.

A large number of drawings concerning bamboo and its by-products have been selected here, particularly basket-ware, but the collection makes no claim to be exhaustive. Each drawing has been chosen on the grounds of originality in regard to the subject – the uses of bamboo. Certain repetitions, however, are intentional, as aesthetic criteria were also part of the decision-making process. For each entry, the engravers' power of observation is an important factor, as well as the composition and precision of these little masterpieces. The laconic nature of the titles has been remedied with *ad hoc* commentaries and references to detail included in other chapters where the subject is given more specific attention. Some other illustrations are included to extend the coverage of the subject: *Essais sur les Tonkinois*, by Gustave Dumoutier (1908), prints from *Imagerie populaire vietnamienne* by Maurice Durand (2011) and photographs by Édouard Hocquard (1892). Wherever possible and available, we have included a more recent photograph to demonstrate the continuity of a technique or an object.

In view of the volume of this sub-part, it is divided into four chapters: the first deals with bamboo used straight after felling, with no further treatment; the second includes sawn but unworked bamboo (i.e. still in tube form); the third chapter concerns bamboo cut into sections and bamboo basket-ware for everyday utensils; and chapter four deals with the Gia Định Art School contribution.

While the uses of and techniques for bamboo have remained the same for more than a century (since 1909), those who handled the various sorts of bamboo are somewhat dissimilar to contemporary Vietnamese, particularly in their clothing.

DOI: 10.4324/9781003350347-8

82 *Bamboo iconography*

This will be an opportunity for the reader to become acquainted with developments in everyday life in Việt Nam. Whenever necessary, an *ad hoc* commentary will inform the reader concerning the changes that have taken place.

Guidelines

Each plate will have:

- A number (for ease of reference).
- The original title in large vernacular characters ("chữ nôm") or occasionally in Chinese characters ("chữ Hán").
- An explanation in small Chinese characters ("chữ Hán"), which, in some cases, follow the title.
- The transcription, in modern Vietnamese ("quốc ngữ") in bold, Roman type, of the title in vernacular characters or, occasionally, in Chinese characters, followed by the English translation in brackets.
- The English translation – in italics – of the eventual explanations in small Chinese characters ("chữ Hán").
- The requisite commentaries.

Note

1 Some details concerning these talented artisan engravers: Nguyễn Văn Đang came from the village of Thanh Liễu, in the canton of Thạch Khôi, Gia Lộc district [in Hải Dương province]. Phạm Trọng Hải was born in the village of Nhân Dục, An Tảo canton, Kim Động district, Hưng Yên province. For Nguyễn Văn Giai and Phạm Văn Tiêu, where they come from is not mentioned in the publication. Source: plate 531, 611, and 651 (Oger, 2009). Not included in Henri Oger's book: Nguyễn Văn Đang's dates are mentioned in *Bách khoa thư bằng tranh*, 1985.

6 Bamboo used as it is, after felling

A bare-chested peasant, wearing wide, calf-length trousers, with his hair in a topknot (see Figure 6.1), is cutting a bamboo shoot with a knife with a blade shaped like a cordyline leaf ("dao bầu"). The bamboo shoot is covered with protective sheaths that have to be removed. The shoot must be cooked in water as often as is necessary to remove some of the natural bitterness – which is more or less pronounced according to the variety – without removing it completely. This does not spoil the flavour of a dish if the cook prepares the dish correctly. Then the bamboo shoot is thinly sliced and stir-fried with beef, pork or chicken. In good harvest seasons, after slicing, surplus bamboo shoots can be dried to preserve them.

When required, they can be softened by soaking in warm water. They can also be preserved by lactic fermentation, which imparts an agreeable, slightly acid taste ("măng chua"). One dish is very popular: bamboo shoots stir-fried with chicken and cashew nuts. Soups simmered with various sorts of bamboo shoots and pig's trotters also have an important place in Vietnamese gastronomy ("chân giò hầm măng").

Figure 6.2 shows a peasant with his head down busy at work: lifting rhizomes with their roots from the base of the bamboo; the rhizomes ensure the underground propagation of the plant. Bamboo also reproduces by seed propagation, but flowering only occurs irregularly (once in every several decades to even once in a century). This is not only a problem for botanists, when they are unable to base identification on a bloom, but especially because flowering coincides with the degeneration of the clump of bamboo and is still nowadays considered to be a "bad omen". Luckily, the plant reproduces and multiplies via its dense clusters of rhizomes. This vegetative propagation is well-regarded by the population, and the plant is not prone to either degeneration or to genetic mutation. On the contrary, it ensures close growth of the bamboo grove, producing a regular harvest of bamboo shoots, which, in the most favourable conditions, can grow up to a metre a day.

Heavy, sharp knife with a thick spine (see Figure 6.3). A "dao rựa" is used to fell the trunk. Here, a peasant dressed in loose clothing with his hair covered with a strip of cloth tied on the top is cutting a felled trunk where the branches have been removed. As noted earlier, it is extremely difficult, if not impossible, to cut bamboo without adequate tools, preferably made of metal. By contrast, a saw is well-adapted for cutting into lengths. The advice noted by Vương Hồng Sển states

DOI: 10.4324/9781003350347-9

84 *Bamboo iconography*

Figure 6.1 **"Cắt măng"** (cutting bamboo shoots). Oger, 1909, p. 206.

that felling should be carried out when there is no moon; when there is moonlight, the bamboo attracts more insect pests.[1]

Dressed in loose clothes and with his hair tied up in a turban ("đội khăn"), this peasant is measuring the surface of a paddy field (see Figure 6.4). The history of measurement in Việt Nam is difficult to document, as central government very rarely made any attempt at standardization. Units of measurement were variable in space and time. The basic unit of length was the joiner's cubit ("thước mộc" 賃木) varying between 0,425 and 0,466m in the 19th century (until 1890), according to various different records. It was used as the basis for calculating the "agrarian thước (thước ruộng 賃坫)". Land areas, written in characters in village archives of the time were expressed in "mẫu" 畝, "sào" (巢,篙), "thước" 賃, "tấc" 掣. One "mẫu" – or 0,36 hectares (1 hectare equals 247 acres) in the 19th century – was equivalent to 10 "sào" or 150 "thước" or 1500 "tấc". The people used the height of bamboo to measure time, which, in the country in the north of Việt Nam, was often counted according to the distance travelled by the sun in the sky. When the sun was about to appear on the horizon, it was "dawn (ban mai)", then "sunrise (hừng đông, reddening to the east)". By then, preparations for work in the paddy fields or for going to market had to be finished. When the sun had risen to the "height of a bamboo pole (mặt trời lên

Bamboo used as it is, after felling 85

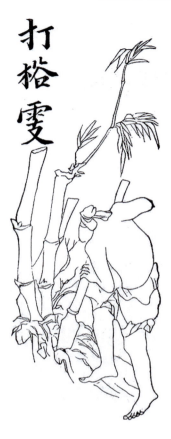

Figure 6.2 **"Đánh gốc tre"** (using a spade to dig up bamboo rhizomes). Oger, 1909, p. 576.

đến một con sào)", it was (already) 9 o'clock and the morning was already well under way. At "two bamboo poles high (mặt trời lên đến hai con sào)", the morning was over, and when "the shadow of the sun stops moving (mặt trời đứng bóng)", the sun was at its zenith at "midday (trưa)" – in other words, "the hour of the Horse (mặt trời đúng ngọ)" – and it was time to seek some shade and shelter from the sun; afternoon began with the descending path of the sun, when the role of bamboo in counting time was less clear, until dusk which often came suddenly. Here, compared to the height of the surveyor, the bamboo pole is less than 3 metres.

The bearded elder (see Figure 6.5) is well dressed – his headwear has flaps reaching to his shoulders that cover his hair, similar to those worn by a Taoist sage; his long, wide robe almost covers his baggy trousers. He wears sandals and leans on a dwarf-bamboo stick; he carries a little pouch on a string.

Figure 6.5 is relevant to 6.6 concerning the succession of the generations in Việt Nam, symbolised here by bamboo: "Tre già, trẻ đã có thì/Còn phần trường chực để tùy người sau (Old and young bamboo each has its time/We will see if the

86   *Bamboo iconography*

Figure 6.3 **"Chặt tre dao rựa"** (cutting bamboo with a large knife). Oger, 1909, p. 647.

descendants continue to carry the torch)".[2] This adage echoes a proverb familiar to Vietnamese and specialists on Việt Nam: "Tre già, măng mọc 椥搽芒木 (Tall bamboo ages, young bamboo shoot grows) ".[3]

Two young women are using carrying poles to transport bundles of bamboo leaves to feed cattle (see Figure 6.7). They are wearing "four panel tunics (áo tứ thân)", usually dyed brown and with the two front panels tied over a full skirt in a dark colour (or black). They are also wearing a white vest undergarment visible at the neckline. Their hair is wrapped in a strip of cloth wound around the head ("vấn khăn"). They are barefoot.[4] As well as the carrying poles for the leafy branches, the taller woman is also shouldering a long-handled sickle for cutting branches

Bamboo used as it is, after felling 87

Figure 6.4 **"Đo ruộng"** (land surveying). Oger, 1909, p. 650.

up to a certain height (permission can be granted for this) without having to fell the bamboo (forbidden if the bamboo does not belong to the young women). The branches are then tied together in bundles. The detail provided in the drawing (and the engraving) is complete and precise, even though the style is very relaxed.

On the first day of the lunar New Year ("mồng một Tết") when there is no moon, evil spirits tend to prowl around the house (see Figure 6.8). In order to discourage them a pole "cây nêu" is erected in front of each dwelling; this bamboo is cut down at the root, its side shoots are removed but a tuft of leaves is retained at the top. Villagers hang various presents (betel, areca-nuts), spiky pineapple leaves and talismans; wind flutes with little bells are also installed to frighten the demons. On the ground under the pole, chalk is used to draw a curved line representing a bow and its bowstring, the arrow being represented by the pole itself.

This "Tết" mast is taken down on the seventh day, to mark the end of the New Year celebrations.

Figure 6.9 is taken from the chapter on "Justice" in the *Essais sur les Tonkinois*.[5] After a long description of the torture of decapitation,[6] the author explains that "in certain cases, after decapitation, the head is exhibited in a public place; it is hung from a tree or a bamboo pole until it has rotted [. . .]". The Imperial regulation made a distinction between a simple beheading ("trảm thủ" 斬首) and beheading

88 Bamboo iconography

Figure 6.5 **"Xã từ lão"** (village elder). Oger, 1909, p. 295.

followed by display ("kiêu thủ" 梟首). "The body is returned to the family when requested; otherwise it is buried in dedicated location. If the family wished to proceed with burial, first of all the head must be sewn back on to the body"[7] before carrying out any other religious ritual. However, it was not always possible to follow this procedure. As the body and the head suffered a different fate, beheading was by far the most serious punishment, the whole body being considered part of the biological heritage bequeathed by the parents, which should be preserved in its entirety.

Bamboo trunks that have been felled in the Upper and Highland Regions, where they grew, are being transported by waterways to the areas where they will be used; thousands of trunks are assembled into compact rafts and floated down river (see Figure 6.10). Here, these huge rafts are taken apart and the trunks bundled together by the dozen to be transported more easily. One man wearing only a loincloth, is still in the shallows, separating the bamboo trunks, while his companion is propping them on a drying trestle, before a woman transports them with a carrying poles.

After the dismantling of the rafts, the bamboo has to be carried to the location where it is needed (see Figure 6.11). Here, a woman wearing the traditional dress

Bamboo used as it is, after felling 89

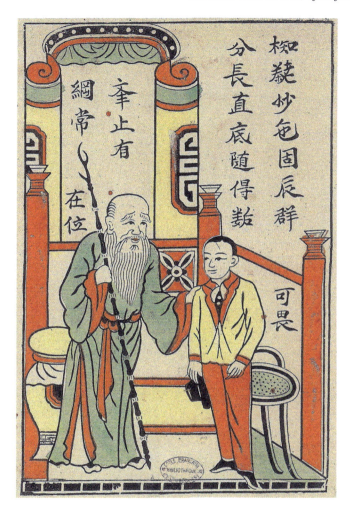

Figure 6.6 Generation gap. Durand, 2011, p. 254.

(tunic with four panels and a skirt with a coloured cloth belt tie) and wearing a wide flat hat is picking up two bundles, each with 20 or so bamboo trunks, probably weighing at least 30 kilos. Presumably, at the other end of the bundles, there is another woman and that these two ladies will carry their load in this way to its destination, a load that would be twice the weight of the bundle on the shoulders of the men in the following illustration.

The bamboo trunks have been felled, trimmed and some have been shortened (see Figure 6.12). They are tied together with cords and lifted to be carried, directly resting on the shoulder. Here, two men are doing this work, dressed in loose clothes, with bare feet; one has his hair in a top knot; the other is wearing a turban. Although

90 *Bamboo iconography*

Figure 6.7 **"Người lấy lá"** (gathering leaves). Oger, 1909, p. 184.

Figure 6.8 **"Nêu trúc"** (bamboo pole for lunar New Year). Oger, 1909, p. 24.

Bamboo used as it is, after felling 91

Figure 6.9 Displaying a head on a bamboo mast after beheading. Dumoutier, 1908, p. 22.

Figure 6.10 **"Dỡ bè"** (dismantling a bamboo raft). Oger, 1909, p. 468.

Figure 6.11 Transporting bundles of large bamboo. Oger, 1909, p. 32.

Figure 6.12 **"Vác tre"** (shouldering bamboo trunks). Oger, 1909, p. 64.

they are viewed from behind, they are portrayed as strong workmen who are used to this kind of work. Their gestures are noted clearly: one is standing straight; the other leans forward, setting the pace.

In Figure 6.13, it is difficult to say whether this is a man or woman. The punter's hair is tied back in a sort of bun. Barefoot (deck shoes didn't exist at the time, and bamboo is slippery when wet), he/she is dressed in a loose robe and wide trousers. The raft is made from bamboo trunks and three bamboo cross bars to keep it flat. The punter is using a pole to propel this simple, unsinkable craft. The raft appears to be trapezoid with the far side slightly wider than the near side: is this an optical illusion or a different spatial awareness?

Figure 6.14 is an ingenious method for assembling bamboo trunks, lengths and bars to make a swing from individual rigid elements: four tall trunks are set in the ground, the upper ends tied together with straps ("lạt"). A length of bamboo rests on the forks of this scaffolding and is tied in place. This upper (horizontal) length is drilled with three large holes which support a second horizontal bar (parallel with the first) assembled to three (vertical) lengths, providing the possibility of a to-and-fro movement. This second bar, also drilled with three holes, bears

Figure 6.13 "**Người đẩy bè**" (punting a bamboo raft). Oger, 1909, p. 462.

94 Bamboo iconography

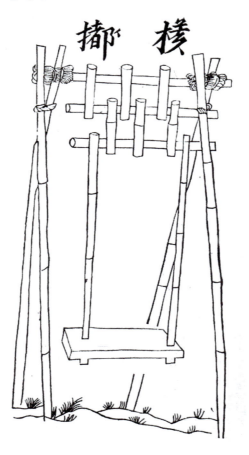

Figure 6.14 **"Cây đu"** ([bamboo], swing, lit.: swing tree). Oger, 1909, p. 96.

three more (vertical) lengths, carrying a third horizontal bar. The swing seat is hung from this lowest bar. The person sitting on the swing can move it with the weight and impetus of the body in a to-and-fro movement (but no lateral movement is possible). By setting in motion the second and the third horizontal bars, the swing can go very high. In village games, the couple who swings the highest wins a prize. The competitors, a man and a woman face to face on the swing, keep the movement going by alternately crouching and standing in rhythm, imitating movement during copulation (initiation rituals concerning fertility are often honoured during village festivals), which is, by the way, suggested by Hồ Xuân Hương's poem *Praise for the swing* (Vịnh leo đu 詠趠擲), written in the 18th century. A panel awards the prize for the best performance. This type of swing is

Bamboo used as it is, after felling   95

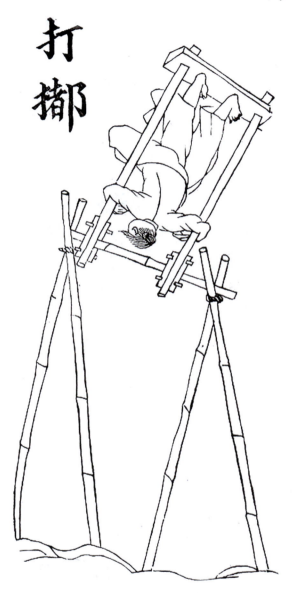

Figure 6.15 A man swinging on his own high in the air (**"đánh đu"**). Oger, 1909, p. 363.

the traditional model used in village jousts and differs from the roundabout swing in the photograph at Hà Nội.

Figure 6.16 is taken from *Essais sur les Tonkinois*, with this commentary: "the swing [. . .] is extremely popular in village festivals, in fact one could say it is

96 *Bamboo iconography*

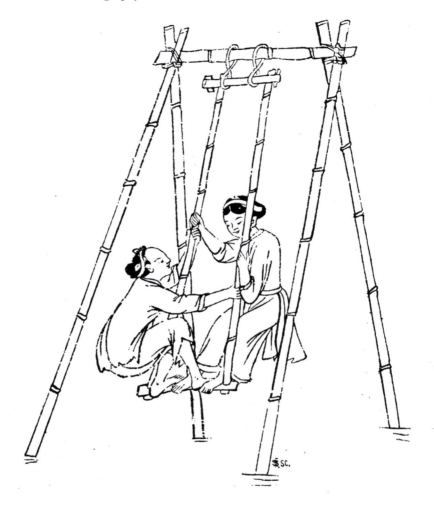

Figure 6.16 Untitled. Dumoutier, 1908, p. 53.

an essential accessory. There is no other cost than the bamboo; even ropes are replaced by lengths of rigid bamboo"[8] (except, perhaps, for the ropes made of strips of bamboo to hold the swing on the gantry).

In his work *Une campagne au Tonkin*, Doctor Hocquard, who was following the French troops, gave the following description of a stronghold and its lookout points (see Figure 6.17):

> The strongholds built in the countryside to defend the approaches to the town are all the same: they are small square redoubts protected by

Bamboo used as it is, after felling 97

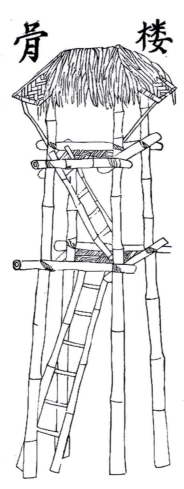

Figure 6.17 **"Lầu cột"** (watchtower). Oger, 1909, p. 481.

crenelated earth walls 2 or 3 meters high; on the inside of the wall a walkway, also earthen, runs round the redoubt and the soldiers stand upon it to fire from the crenels.

At each of the four corners of the stronghold, there is a mirador with a thatched roof that somewhat overhangs the stronghold wall; this is where the sentries were posted to observe the terrain. It is difficult to imagine how a man could remain for hours in such a flimsy shelter, so cramped that he cannot lie down and so low that he had to stay crouched. The pole supports are so long and thin that they must have swayed with the sentry's every movement; he would be standing like a cockerel on its perch, balancing on the five or six widely spaced, horizontal bamboo struts placed by way of a floor.

A wood engraving illustrated this text.[9]

This gutter is made from a bamboo trunk split lengthwise with the diaphragms removed, then placed on supports made from two bamboo trunks tied together and spread out to act as trestles. Note the odd shape of the rainwater butt: its upper edge is drawn as if seen from above and its base is represented from the front by a straight line. The two ends of the gutter are on perpendicular planes and in conical

Figure 6.18 "**Máng hứng nước**" (rain gutter). Oger, 1909, p. 181.

projection, whereas they should be parallel. This is a consequence of the draughtsmen engravers' notion of perspective.

The gutter shown on its own in Figure 6.19 gives the reader a clearer idea of this rendering of perspective.

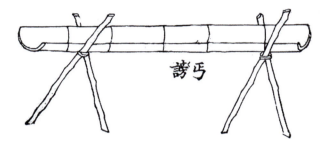

Figure 6.19 "**Cái máng**" (gutter or conduit). Oger, 1909, p. 414.

Figure 6.20 (*People living by the coast use stilts to move around whatever the tides*, this is the meaning of the expression in vernacular **đi kheo**). Oger, 1909, p. 88.

Figure 6.21 **"Bổ nhà lầu"** (making a new roof). Oger, 1909, p. 637.

See commentary for Figure 6.18. In spite of the distortion in the drawing, the water will run out as required. That is the essential result.

In Figure 6.20, the man on stilts has his hair tied up in a cloth on the crown of his head; he is wearing a wide tunic over baggy, knee-length trousers gathered in at the knee. He is gripping the bamboo trunk between his big toe and the second toe to hold on to the stilts. The absence of any foot support allows for a more elastic gait as the feet are "as one" with the stilts.

Bamboo used as it is, after felling 101

Figure 6.22 **"Bán thang tre"** (bamboo ladder seller). Oger, 1909, p. 85.

Dressed only in a loincloth, the roofer in Figure 6.21 has climbed onto the roof using a bamboo ladder. He is covering the roof with thatch or with sugar cane leaves.

The bamboo ladder seller is carrying two in this drawing; they are tied to the rod used as a carrying pole. He is wearing a turban made from a strip of cloth in the shape of an axe blade ("khăn đầu rìu") wound around his head. His loose, open tunic has no buttons and falls from one bare shoulder. He is walking barefoot, as do most peasants.

A peasant woman is crossing over a narrow stream on a footbridge made from a wide bamboo trunk placed on a trestle made of two crossed bamboo poles, held

102 *Bamboo iconography*

Figure 6.23 **"Qua lần cầu"** (bridge for continuing on the way). Oger, 1909, p. 323.

together with a tie. She is holding a bamboo handrail with her right hand. With her left hand, she is holding a heavy basket of goods (grain or rice) balanced on her head, and over this, she has a wide, flat hat made of Chinese fan palm leaves ("nón ba tầm"). The drawing clearly indicates the decisive movements of the young woman crossing the footbridge as quickly as possible. The slightest hesitation would make the crossing riskier.

The sight of a young peasant woman doing her washing from a pontoon over the edge of a village pond ("cầu ao") is a common event. The pontoon is made from four bamboo trunks resting on two cross bars held firmly in place by two thick

Bamboo used as it is, after felling 103

Figure 6.24 Woman doing her washing from a bamboo pontoon. Oger, 1909, p. 58.

vertical lengths of bamboo set in the pond bed on either side of the pontoon. The bank end of the pontoon rests directly on the ground.

This set of bladed weapons, known as "lỗ bộ", has an unusual feature (see Figure 6.25): all the weapons illustrated have a shaft made of bamboo (except for the "tay thước", a single piece of wood). The title suggests its location: the guardroom at the townhall. The "thiết linh (nunchaku or chainsticks)" was originally a flail for threshing rice and has become a dangerous weapon now sometimes included in military training arms drill.

Figure 6.26 provides interesting information on bamboo technology: how to imprint a permanent curve on a bamboo trunk. Its elasticity means that, when pressure is released, it tends to revert to its original shape. As with rattan, heat

104 *Bamboo iconography*

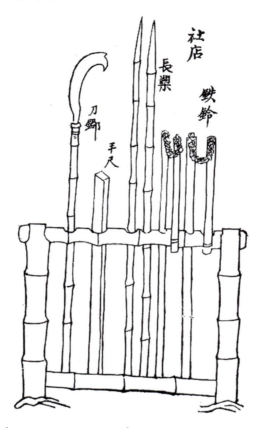

Figure 6.25 "*Xã điếm*" (town hall); "**Dao quắm**" (slash-hook)/"**Tay thước**" (type of cudgel used as an offensive weapon[10]); "Trường sóc" (long lance); "Thiết linh (nunchaku)", chainsticks. Oger, 1909, p. 7.

or fire can be used to effect a curve. Here, a peasant, wearing a turban with two knots ("khăn đầu rìu") and loose clothes is bending a bamboo trunk wedged between a pile of bricks and a cross bar made from trunks set firmly in the earth. Under the end of the bamboo to be bent, a small fire has been lit. This will allow the bamboo to be given a permanent curve. A straight stick thus becomes a weapon with a fearsome "hook (câu liêm)" that can tip a mahout off his elephant.

In the case of Figure 6.27, there is no need to bend a bamboo pole to make a hook. All that is necessary is choosing a pole with a branch that can be cut to make a hook. And the result is a simple, practical, reliable tool.

Bamboo used as it is, after felling   105

Figure 6.26 **"Uốn gậy tre"** (bending a length of bamboo). Oger, 1909, p. 544.

106 *Bamboo iconography*

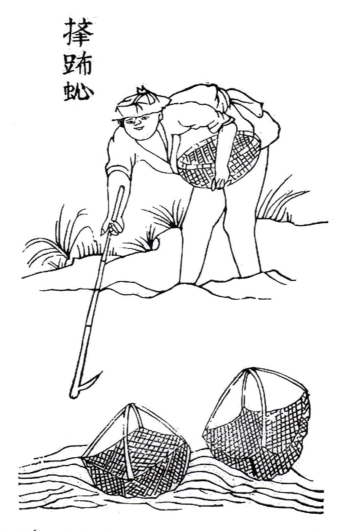

Figure 6.27 **"Cất vó tôm"** (lifting a shrimping net [using a hooked stick]). Oger, 1909, p. 397.

Notes

1 Vương Hồng Sển, 1993, p. 633.
2 Durand, 2011, p. 254, modified translation.
3 *Nam quốc phương ngôn tục ngữ bị lục*, f ° 14b.
4 For the dress of Vietnamese peasants in the early 20th century, the reader is advised to consult the descriptions in the exhibition catalogue of *Hà Nội en couleurs, 1914–1917: autochromes des archives de la planète* (Đinh & Poisson, 2014). The autochromes

developed by Léon Busy for the "Archives de la Planète" were more or less contemporary with the plates by Oger.

5 Dumoutier, 1908, p. 22.
6 *Ibidem*, pp. 20–1.
7 *Ibidem*, p. 23.
8 Dumoutier, 1908, p. 53.
9 Hocquard, 1892, pp. 96–7.
10 Génibrel, 1898, p. 860.

7 Uses of bamboo tube

Her dress identifies this woman as a farmer: she is wearing a belt tied around the waist of her tunic (see Figure 7.1). She has a conical hat and is using a flail composed of two sticks – one, short and the other, long. The short flail is connected to the long flail by a chain, or, as in this engraving, by a length of bamboo. The short flail strikes the soya pods, crushing them to extract the beans.

Bamboo tubes have many uses, such as protection for an important missive[1] or carrying necessities (water for example). But tubes have other, sometimes surprising uses: here, as a float (see Figure 7.2). If the diaphragms are retained at each end of the bamboo tube, it is completely closed and can behave as a float. Then, tied to the arms and legs, they can prevent the child from drowning. However, this drawing is somewhat naïve: one single float attached to only one of the child's legs would have the effect of unbalancing the child in the water!

In Figure 7.3, the artist has added some interesting detail: metal chains and straps that hold the cangue firmly together. The number 783 is inscribed on one of the cross bars, probably the prisoner's identity number. The legs of the figure have not been included in the drawing. He seems to be smiling and is carrying his cangue rather jauntily.

All (the prisoners) carry [. . .] a cangue made from two lengths of bamboo measuring 60 or 70 centimetres long and joined with two cross pieces. The head is imprisoned between these two rigid bars, one in front and one behind the neck, while each bamboo pole rests on a shoulder. It is similar to a short ladder in between whose rungs the convict has passed his head and whose uprights rest on his shoulders. The cangues carried by the prisoners are made of green wood and are quite light; they are called travelling cangues because they are worn by criminals when they are transferred from one prison to another. As well as this model, there are three other sorts of cangue described in the vietnamese code (*Hoàng Việt luật lệ* 皇越律例 enacted in 1813 by Gia Long, first emperor of the Nguyễn dynasty) in the chapter on punishments under the names of *small, medium and large cangue*. The latter is very heavy; it is reinforced at each end with large iron rings.[2]

DOI: 10.4324/9781003350347-10

Figure 7.1 Threshing soya beans with a bamboo flail. (Described in the vernacular by the expression **đập đậu tương.**) Oger, 1909, p. 252.

In spite of an effeminate appearance, the person in Figure 7.4 is a man, and too well dressed to be a peasant. Although some country women smoke a straight bamboo pipe ("điếu cày", ploughman's pipe) it is not a common practice. In town, ladies do smoke a bowl-shaped pipe (or tube, "điếu bát, điếu ống"), extended with a long bamboo stalk so that they do not have to hold the tube directly with the lips in an inelegant manner.

However, the details of the dress do not show the difference between a man and a woman – even to the practised Vietnamese eye. The long tunic with a narrow collar has a side fastening; the trousers are wide; the feet bare. The hair is tied up in a bun on the back of the head. Women do not sit like this, buttocks directly on the ground, like a dog (except when working or at the market).

A ball of tobacco is placed in the bowl that has been inserted into the bamboo tube ("nõ điếu"). The smoker lights the pipe using a spill, usually a thin strip of

110   *Bamboo iconography*

Figure 7.2 Child wearing a bamboo float to avoid drowning. Oger, 1909, p. 675.

Figure 7.3 **"Người tù"** (a prisoner [carrying a cangue]). Oger, 1909, p. 33.

Uses of bamboo tube 111

Figure 7.4 **"Hút điếu cầy"** ([man] smoking a water pipe). Oger, 1909, p. 493.

thoroughly dry bamboo, "cái đóm", "que đóm" or "đóm diêm" (see Figures 8.9–10). Note that the internodes of the bamboo are wider at the top end of the pipe. The diaphragm at lowest internode has been retained so that a little water remains in the base. The diaphragms at the other internodes have been removed. The pipe bowl, made of wood, is inserted into a hole bored in the tube.

Figure 7.5 shows the "luxury" version of the peasant pipe. The green surface bark of the pipe body has been scratched and inscribed with decorative motifs. The wooden pipe bowl is rimmed with metal. A moveable foot made with a single, bent bamboo

112   *Bamboo iconography*

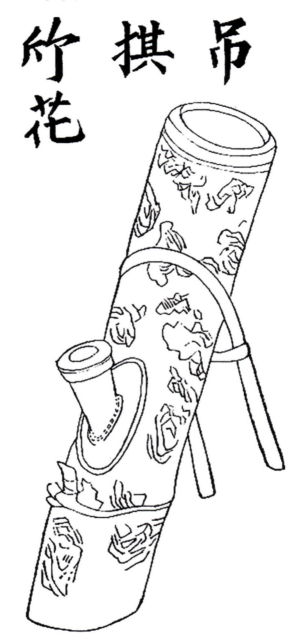

竹 掑 吊
花

Figure 7.5 **"Điếu cầy trúc hoa"** (decorated water pipe). Oger, 1909, p. 476.

Uses of bamboo tube 113

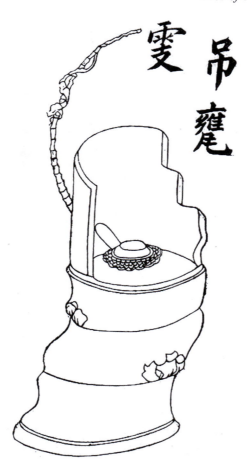

Figure 7.6 **"Điếu ống tre"** (pipe [in the shape of a] "tube", made from an old bamboo trunk). Oger, 1909, p. 546.

stem is held in place with a tie; this keeps the pipe stable. Without it, the pipe would roll on the ground and could not be kept in place. It is strictly taboo to spill even a tiny amount of water from this pipe – and not only because of the horrible smell.

Here, the top opening of the pipe is drawn as if seen from above and is out of perspective in relation to the foot represented as if viewed on the level. The intention of the draughtsman is unclear.

The model of pipe above is in the shape of a cylinder but, as it is made from a very old root of bamboo, its contours are bulbous and irregular, with the traces of

114 *Bamboo iconography*

Figure 7.7 **"Khoan xe điếu rễ trúc"** (drilling the stem of a pipe made of old dwarf bamboo). Oger, 1909, p. 191.

the "three stars (tam tinh)" side-shoots still visible. Three short, close internodes are visible. A sort of screen has been added to the top of the pipe to protect the flame from draughts when it is being lit.

This element is made of rosewood and may be decorated with mother of pearl inlay. The smoker breathes in the smoke using the length of tube made from a stalk of dwarf bamboo. The base of the object contains water, making a clearly audible gurgle – the sign of a good pipe.

Figures 7.7 and 7.8 show the technique for piercing the diaphragms in a long stalk of old dwarf bamboo in order to make a pipe stem for the model shown in the previous illustration or for the bowl-shaped model. The stem is held straight; otherwise, the gimlet could pierce the stalk rather than the diaphragms. The well-dressed artisan, his hair tied up in a bun and covered with a turban, is holding a gimlet (probably metal, a straight rigid wire) in his hands and is rolling it to pierce

Figure 7.8 **"Khoan xe điếu tay tre"** (piercing the diaphragm of a bamboo by hand to make a pipe stem; note that the word order in the caption in "nôm" should have been inversed: khoan tay xe điếu tre). Oger, 1909, p. 238.

the inside of the stalk. This is a delicate operation requiring dexterity and concentration. The result can be further improved by adding sand applied using a rod, turning it between the palms evenly and continuously. The artisan's stool, shown here as trapezoid, is in danger of tipping at any moment.

To make a blowpipe, one must first choose a strong compact bamboo so that once the stalk is straightened, it remains in shape and does not bend (see Figure 7.9). Dwarf bamboo is usually chosen. Then the diaphragms must be perforated, a delicate task undertaken by this artisan who, having hollowed out the core of the bamboo, is widening and polishing the interior so that nothing obstructs the projectile.

To this end, the artisan is rubbing the inside of the tube with a wire coated with sand and held in place by two stakes set in the ground. The sand, glued to the wire, acts like emery paper. The dried leaves of *Streblus asper* ("cây duối"), with their rough surface, can also be used to polish the inside of pipes.

From her dress, we may assume that this is a woman on her way to buy a dog: she has tied up her four-panel tunic with a belt (see Figure 7.10). The utensil she is

116   Bamboo iconography

Figure 7.9 **"Thông ống xì đồng trúc"** (hollowing a bamboo tube to make a blowpipe). Oger, 1909, p. 692

carrying on her shoulder is a slip-knot that she will fix round the animal's neck. It will be adjusted to the right size; otherwise, she might strangle the dog. The slip-knot serves as a lead, but a detail is underlined in the drawing: the cord is threaded through a perforated bamboo tube (using a technique described in the fabrication of a pipe stem).

In Figure 7.11, the reason for this is clearly evident.

Docteur Hocquard, an army doctor in Hà Nội at the time of the Tonkin conquest in mid-1884, took series of photographs on everyday life there, including this albumen print series on "The Dog Market" (see Figure 7.12). His photographs are the perfect illustrations for his commentaries:

> Very close to the citadel, at the beginning of Basket Street (*rue des Paniers*) the edible dog market is held every fifth day. The smallest animals for sale

Figure 7.10 **"Mua chó"** (dog merchant). Oger, 1909, p. 304.

are presented in large loosely woven baskets, rather similar to the type of coop for protecting chickens raised in the French countryside. The dogs that are too old to be kept in this sort of cage are kept on a lead threaded through a length of bamboo; the bamboo allows the dog to be kept at a distance and to prevent it from biting.[3]

The explanation provided by the doctor is only valid when one is leading the dog after the sale, but does not explain why the bamboo would be retained once the dog is tied up at home. Indeed the bamboo tube is useful for keeping an unruly dog at a distance, but it is also useful in preventing the animal from biting through its lead and taking the path to . . . freedom!

118 *Bamboo iconography*

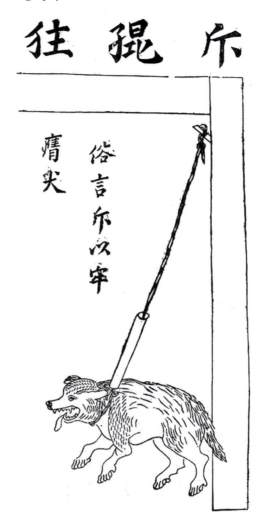

Figure 7.11 **"Xích con chó"** (putting a dog on a leash). ([Whence] the vernacular "tying (**xích**) a dog in a kennel".) Oger, 1909, p. 574.

The perforation of the diaphragms of bamboo trunks with a wider diameter is relatively easy. This craftsman is doing so by using a length of thinner bamboo sharpened to a point (see Figure 7.13). The diaphragm is the least resistant part of the trunk. However, if it is not disturbed, it remains resistant for the useful life of the bamboo; used as a container, it is unthinkable that such a utensil might leak due to a blemish. When the perforation of the diaphragm is not necessary, it is retained

Figure 7.12 **"Le marché aux chiens"** (the dog market). 1884. ANOM. Photograph by Charles-Edouard Hocquard.

at the internodes (for example, when the bamboo is used as a pillar in building work), as the diaphragm contributes to the rigidity of the trunk.

Figure 7.14 is an ambivalent object: imitation bamboo being used as a drinking vessel. A bamboo trunk can always be cut into a length with the diaphragm retained and then be used as a cup. In this case, the bamboo leaf motif indicates that this is an artefact, not raw bamboo. The imitation of a mature bamboo trunk and the representation of a knotty branch with "three stars" internodes for a handle can be interpreted as a discreet homage to Nature on the part of the ceramist. The caption of Figure 7.15 (a teapot) is more explicit.

This teapot that looks as if it were picked straight out of a clump of bamboo confirms the ceramist's respect and praise of Nature (see Figure 7.15). The handle and the spout imitate the knotty branches of bamboo, sprouting from two different internodes and therefore respecting the alternate side shoot growth pattern of real bamboo. This is a case where the craftsman, finding Nature to be perfect and beautiful, produces an everyday utensil that is simply imitation of bamboo in its natural state.

The drawing of this child's toy is incomplete and does not provide an understanding of the mechanism for firing the dart (see Figure 7.16). A tube with diaphragm has a slit on one side to set a peg by way of a "trigger", which is made of a

120 *Bamboo iconography*

Figure 7.13 **"Thông ống đứa (nứa)"** (perforating a bamboo trunk to make a tube). Oger, 1909, p. 688.

piece of bent bamboo. The peg is pressed down when the dart is placed in the tube. The dart is fired when the spring, made of the piece of bent bamboo, is released. The dart can reach a distance of a dozen metres and can hurt but it can only fire one dart at a time and needs to be constantly reloaded. There are, nowadays, many variants of this device, where a rubber band can be used as a spring.

A medicine man, wearing a turban, is seated informally on the ground fanning the fire by blowing through a tube to "burn sections of dwarf bamboo to collect the sap", which is running into a bowl. Known as "trúc lịch",[4] the decoction produced in this way is used as medication in Chinese medicine and/or in folk medicine in Việt Nam, with the same effect as an expectorant or a febrifuge (see Figure 7.17). Young bamboo shoots rich in sap are chosen and heated over

Uses of bamboo tube 121

Figure 7.14 **"Cái chén"** (a cup). **"Cái chén làm hình ống trúc"** (a cup in the shape of bamboo). Oger, 1909, p. 256.

Figure 7.15 **"Cái ấm đất hình ống trúc"** (imitation bamboo earthenware teapot). Oger, 1909, p. 135.

Figure 7.16 **"Bắn súng tre"** ([child] firing a bamboo gun). Oger, 1909, p. 221.

the fire to extract the sap, which is collected and then drunk mixed with ginger or mothers' milk, according to age, by children: it is used as a cure for voice loss, fever or constipation.

Ducks raised for the pot in Việt Nam undergo treatments that would outrage many animal rights supporters (see Figure 7.18). At the market, before buying a live duck, it is advisable to first feel its gizzard, in case a dishonest tradesman has inserted the cheap option of a potato in its place. To prepare a dish of duck blood

Figure 7.17 **"Đốt trúc lịch làm thang thuốc"** (burning pieces of bamboo to prepare a decoction). Oger, 1909, p. 616.

curd ("tiết canh vịt"), the beak is chopped off and the stream of blood is collected in a bowl until it runs dry. The animal does not die immediately and can still run around – even bleed dry. To facilitate plucking, the cook simply makes a small incision in the skin of the bird's neck and blows into it using a bamboo tube. He can then remove the small feathers that would not be visible otherwise.

This technique is not to be confused with blowing into the neck of the bird that is already dead and prepared with spices – for the Peking Duck recipe – when the skin is then detached by roasting.

Figure 7.19 is taken from the Oger collection, put together a year later from the wood engravings in *Essais sur les Tonkinois* by Gustave Dumoutier.[7] A street seller, seated on the ground, is blowing through a bamboo tube into a ball of transparent molasses (called "mật", but not necessarily made from honey, which is more

124　*Bamboo iconography*

Figure 7.18 **"Thổi cổ vịt dễ làm lông ống"** (blowing into a duck's throat to facilitate plucking). Oger, 1909, p. 618.

expensive); he is blowing through the bamboo tube held in his left hand and, with his right hand, he shapes the animal as he blows. A long text, in Chinese and in vernacular writing, comments on the scene. To the side of the molasses pan are two shapes on sticks ready to be sold; once they have cooled, they keep their shape. Two woven bamboo baskets are used to transport the goods.

The commentary of Figure 7.20 reads: "On a small portable table, itinerant confectioners make blown sugar sweets in the shape of birds and animals. These treats are a delight for the children; they are called "hàng kéo gà". To make nougats, The Annam people cook and reduce molasses with starch or sticky rice flour to which they add almonds. They also make marshmallows".[8] Dumoutier

Uses of bamboo tube 125

Figure 7.19 Cooking molasses[5] to make transparent jelly [paste] sweets, called **kẹo**[6] in the vernacular. Blowing through a bamboo tube with a ball of this paste on the end to make jelly animal shapes as toys for children. Oger, 1909, p. 338.

Figure 7.20 This drawing has the title "Blown sugar sweets seller". Dumoutier, 1908, p. 193.

126 *Bamboo iconography*

Figure 7.21–22 "**Hàng kẹo kéo**" (drawn sugar sweets seller). The two signatures on the drawings are those of Nguyễn Tường Tam. 1925. Coyaud, 1980, p. 10.

did not make clear that these were three different tradesmen, although they are all sweet sellers for children: on the drawing, the confectioner carries his merchandise in two woven bamboo baskets; he is sitting on his carrying pole on the ground and is blowing the sweets through his tube and shaping them with his left hand watched by a delighted child; this is "hàng kéo gà". The second peddler mentioned by Dumoutier is selling drawn nougat; his transportable display case is placed on a trestle; the buyer places his bet; the seller turns the roulette, which stops at a number corresponding to the length of the nougat won by the child; this is "hàng kẹo kéo" (in fact, it is always the same quantity of nougat that is served; it is just that the peddler draws it out further so that there seems to be more of it, whence the name "kẹo kéo" – drawn sweet). This seller also may offer marshmallow that he cuts up using big scissors. The engraver of the Dumoutier

Uses of bamboo tube 127

Figures 7.21–22 (Continued)

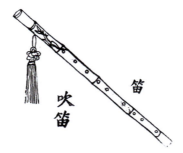

Figure 7.23 **"Thổi sáo"/"sáo"** (playing a flute/flute). Oger, 1909, p. 177.

128 *Bamboo iconography*

Figure 7.24 No caption. (Musician playing a side-blown flute.) Oger, 1909, p. 183.

illustrations has a very free but also precise hand, and his style is quite dissimilar to that (or those) in Oger's plates.

This is a drawing of "hàng kẹo kéo", by Mai Thứ, dated 1925, and a manuscript text concerning travelling salesmen by De Fénis, with the assistance of Nguyễn Tường Tam,[9] who was a student at ESBAI (Ecole supérieure des beaux-arts de l'Indochine) in the first year of its existence, who went on field work with his classmates (see Figures 7.21–22).[10]

Only the wind instruments made of bamboo in Việt Nam are detailed on pages 127 and 128. Some of them, such as the mouth organ and the "khene", played by some ethnic minorities, are made of reed tubes rather than bamboo, as reed is lighter in weight. However, the wind instrument most often played in the so-called "learned" traditional music is the side-blown flute ("sáo trúc" – bamboo flute – also called "địch"), whereas the end-blown flute ("tiêu"), similar to the Japanese "shakuhachi", is not played so frequently. The use of the "trúc" variety of bamboo is so common that the instrument is often simply called by the name of the plant, particularly in poetry; so, while "tiếng tơ" means music played on stringed instruments (with strings made from silk), "tiếng trúc" means music played on flutes (made of bamboo).

The scholarly dress of this flute player indicates that he is playing a piece from the learned corpus (early 20th century). Nowadays, bamboo is used to make numerous wind instruments generally described as "sáo Mèo" ("Hmông wind instruments").

Figure 7.25 shows a bamboo stake for displaying a notice. The stake is square in section and is shown next to a bamboo branch used as a spring for a snare. The reason for this strange association of objects is unclear. The ban on urination is engraved directly on the bamboo, which is rare, as normally this would be written

Uses of bamboo tube 129

Figure 7.25 "*Chiêu đề*" (*Notice*. It is forbidden to urinate here). Oger, 1909, p. 633.

on paper and pasted onto the stake, whether it concerned a judgement or a prohibition (as in the case of a stake set next to a convict); however, sometimes characters were engraved directly on the bark of the bamboo itself. The green bark becomes yellow as it dries, but the habit of referring to such inscriptions as "sử xanh" (green history) endured because of the origin of the bamboo tablets and also certainly to insist on the permanent timeliness of the history in question.

130 *Bamboo iconography*

Figure 7.26 **"Trát chum tương"** (sealing a jar for soya sauce). Oger, 1909, p. 256.

This drawing shows the final stage of the preparation of "tương", a Vietnamese soya sauce, which is light brown and lumpy (not to be confused with what is more commonly available in shops as "soya sauce", a smooth dark brown liquid).

The recipe for this sauce is complicated: first of all, it involves cooking sticky rice, which is then left to moulder (on large flat trays and respecting particular conditions of heat and humidity) and then it is mixed with toasted soya beans. This the final stage is the sealing of the "tương" in jars so that the sauce can ferment over a long period of time without souring or being spoilt by any foreign

Figure 7.27 **"Nồi nước rửa"** (cauldron for rinsing water). Oger, 1909, p. 236.

bodies. A terracotta – or, better still, ceramic – jar is used as a container. It is left outside in all weathers. The jar is supported on bamboo poles tied round with rope to prevent the wind or the rain from upsetting the precious condiment. The jar is caulked with a mixture of mud and chopped straw to protect it from flies and maggots. The athletic young woman in the illustration is carrying out this procedure.

In the north of Việt Nam, several well-known villages – such as Cự Đà, on the banks of the river Nhuệ, in Thanh Oai district, and Bần, in Mỹ Hào district – specialize in this activity. There is also a strong family tradition for preparing this condiment, which builds the reputation of certain housewives. The celebrated 18th-century Vietnamese physician Lê Hữu Trác included several recipes in his compendium *Nữ công thắng lãm* 女工勝覽 [Comprehensive Overview of Women's Work].[11] Another early-20th-century recipe was recorded by the wife of the Scholar, Trần Lê Nhân, in 1945, at Vĩnh Yên, and passed on to Đinh Trọng Hiếu's

132 *Bamboo iconography*

mother. In this text, it is recommended to ferment the "tương" in the jar for several consecutive moons; spoiling the sauce implied not only the ruin of the family but was a serious dishonour. In general, spoiling the fermentation was considered as serious as spoiling mayonnaise in France.

At least part of the title (see Figure 7.27) is inappropriate here: the "cauldron" (nồi) is unnecessary for rinsing water which does not need to be heated. "Chum", water jar, would be more appropriate and is a familiar object all over Việt Nam, in all sizes and (almost) all shapes (oval, cylindrical, tapering, necked). Here, the jar is loosely wedged between lengths of bamboo set in the ground.

A ladle made of a coconut shell with a handle inserted and fixed through two holes is used to scoop out the water. A jar like this is placed at the entrance to a courtyard (for rinsing off the mud from the roadway) or in a discreet corner for washing but always placed so that ablutions also serve to water the surrounding plants.

Notes

1 See *supra*, Chapter 5, pp. 72–74.
2 Hocquard, 1892, p. 66. The cangue was not in the list of the Five Punishments in the *Hoàng Việt luật lệ*. In the preliminary part of the code, and not in the chapter on punishments, it was considered more as an instrument of torture, restricting the movements of the offenders during their trial and then during all their time in prison awaiting sentence. *Hoàng Việt luật lệ* 皇越律例, book I, fᵒˢ 42a-b in *The Vietnamese Nôm Preservation Foundation* [Accessed: 2/02/2020].
3 Hocquard, 1892, pp. 176–8.
4 "Lịch 歷" and not "tịch 夕" as mistakenly written by the author.
5 Mistakenly, the author only mentions molasses ("mật"), whereas it is a mixture of molasses and pea flour.
6 "Kẹo" 糩 and not "keo" 膠 as stated by the author.
7 Dumoutier, 1908, p. 193.
8 *Ibidem*, figure 77.
9 Future author in the "Self-Reliant Literary Association (Tự Lực Văn Đoàn)", under the pen name Nhất Linh.
10 Coyaud, 1980, p. 12.
11 Lê Hữu Trác, [1971], pp. 70–7.

8 Use of split bamboo cut into lengths

The first requirement of a fence is to prevent the intrusion of burglars, bandits and wild animals (see Figure 8.1). To be efficient, the fence must present a danger to dissuade the intruder. Varieties of bamboo that can be cut to provide sharp edges, particularly "nứa", are used to this end, "nứa" being preferred not for its strength but for its fearsome cutting edge. The artisan further improves this quality by splitting and sharpening each length to a point. Two peasants are building the fence, one bare-chested, the other fully dressed: they have set "nứa" stakes in the ground and are tying them to cross bars made from bamboo trunks that have been split in two to hold the fence firmly in place. In the foreground, the man is using a "knife in the shape of a cordyline leaf (dao bầu)" to split the "nứa". Behind him, the other man is setting a stake in the ground.

Only the shade placed on the four posts is made of woven bamboo basket-ware (see Figure 8.2). The matting the sleeper is lying on is probably made of reeds ("chiếu cói") or perhaps crushed bamboo stalks. The shade is placed on four posts; these four branches have been chosen, in this case, for their fork. The shade is simply resting on the posts and can be easily removed and put back.

In Figure 8.3, the moveable screen is made from strong, woven bamboo; it is placed by the door of the house to provide shade from the sun or to prevent passers-by from seeing inside. It is a sort of mobile door, so it is made from top quality bamboo, usually the cortical part ("tre cật"). The open parts with no vertical weave are used to hang clothes so that they can be taken off behind the screen and put on again quickly.

The drawing (see Figure 8.4) should not be taken as a model! However, it is clearly useful for understanding building methods and the materials needed for the frame, which is made of four wattle fences held in place in a rectangle by the hooks of the sturdy posts set in the ground. The clumps of earth filling the framework are closely tamped. The plinth is completed when a bamboo rack has been placed on the top. In wet areas, the framework is built differently, particularly if used for consolidating dykes.[1]

Made of bamboo slats, the simple pen (see Figure 8.5) is made for restraining ducks, who are so close together that they are free neither to move around nor to break out of the enclosure. This structure is woven on the ground with widely spaced slats, and the resulting rectangle of basketwork is rolled round and tied to the required size using strong straps ("dây lạt"). The agitated movement of the

DOI: 10.4324/9781003350347-11

134 *Bamboo iconography*

Figure 8.1 **"Rào giậu"** (fence). Oger, 1909, p. 347.

ducks in the confined space tends to divert the attention of the reader from the (intended?) awkward draughtsmanship of the structure.

There are two reasons for the inclusion of Figure 8.6 in a work on bamboo. Firstly, because bamboo leaves are necessary for the fumigation but also because this strange installation is now no longer used because it is too complicated.

The support placed on the ground ("cái rế tre"), should hold a large cauldron (not featured here) in which six or seven sorts of leaves have been brewed (these can be found in the garden or can be bought in packets at the market, ready to use). A low frame made of two bamboo trunks supported by four short pillars (the two in the background are missing in the drawing) is in place over the cauldron. A naked man is sitting on this, concealed by a cylindrical bamboo screen that is just the

Use of split bamboo cut into lengths 135

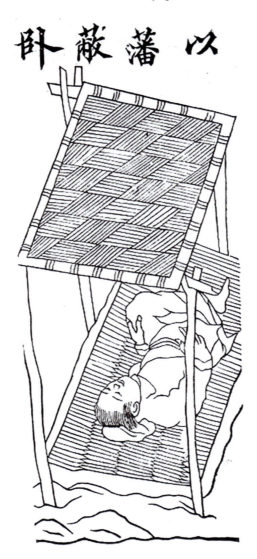

Figure 8.2 "*Dĩ phiên tề ngọa*" (taking a nap under a woven shade). Oger, 1909, p. 272.

width of the cauldron. A sheet is placed over the top so that the fumigation can have an effect on the patient. The artist has opened out a panel of the cover so that we can see the patient.

Nowadays, the procedure is less complicated: the patient, shrouded with a thick cover, inhales the aromatic steam from the boiling cauldron placed just in front of him.

136 *Bamboo iconography*

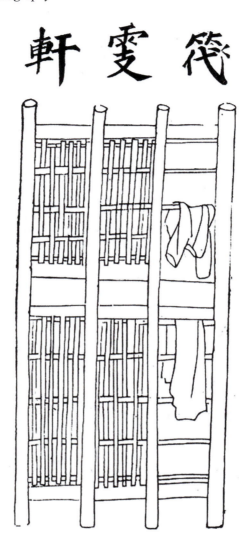

Figure 8.3 **"Dại che hiên"** (screen for veranda). Oger, 1909, p. 575.

This is considered the best remedy for chills. The tried and trusted mixtures of herbs for fumigation were formulated to dilate the pores and eliminate toxins (*Ageratum conyzoïdes* L., Asteracea – "cây cứt lợn" – and *Artemisia vulgaris* L., Composite – "cây ngải cứu"), whereas currently, leaves with menthol essential oils are preferred for their antibacterial and expectorant properties (*Ocimum sanctum* L. – "lá hương nhu tía"; *Mentha arvensis* L. – "lá bạc hà"; *Perilla ocymoïdes* L. – "lá tía tô" – all three of which are Labiates).

Use of split bamboo cut into lengths 137

Figure 8.4 **"Thổ khối trúc thành bệ"** (earth tamped in a bamboo frame for making a plinth base). Oger, 1909, p. 13.

Figure 8.5 **"Quây nuôi vịt"** (enclosure for raising ducks). Oger, 1909, p. 205.

138 *Bamboo iconography*

Figure 8.6 **"Xông nước lá"** (fumigation using a decoction of leaves). Oger, 1909, p. 550.

The leaves of bamboo, grapefruit and citronella are invariably used as the basis of these preparations.

The two pig butchers in Figure 8.7 are bare-chested and have their hair tied up in a topknot. One is seated on a low bamboo platform and holds the animal, carefully trussed with three ropes and a bamboo trunk, immobilizing all four legs, so that the pig is deprived of all movement. The other butcher slits the jugular vein with the knife in the shape of a cordyline ("dao bầu") leaf, while, with his left hand, he grips the pig's snout so that it cannot bite or squeal. The blood is collected in a basin. The drawing deforms perspective, probably unintentionally, unless the engraver happens to prefer trapezoid furniture and basins with a reduced base. Otherwise, the draughtsmanship is clear in so far as it describes the plump butcher, his muscly mate and their precise gestures.

"Đình liệu" is another name for this bundle of bamboo used to illuminate public spaces by the communal house during evening meetings (see Figure 8.8).

Use of split bamboo cut into lengths 139

Figure 8.7 "*Sát trư*" (killing a pig). Oger, 1909, p. 424.

The torch can be daubed with resin, which is only necessary to get the torch lit, because afterwards, the rest of it will burn down completely with no problem if the bamboo is properly dry. A peasant is watching the torch burn while holding the flames at a distance with a prop.

Figure 8.9 shows a scholar wearing a turban and dressed in a long robe and wide, ankle-length trousers. The subject is putting a spill back into a large bamboo container fixed on the pillar of a house (or maybe a public building). The spills are prepared using the inner layer of bamboo, where the fibres are soft and spongy – a cheap material that is cut into thin strips and dried. The spill is lit and burns until the flame end is stubbed out by crushing it on the ground. If the remaining part is long enough to be reused, it is placed in the length of bamboo trunk provided to hold the spills.

In his *Categorized Sayings from the library* Lê Quý Đôn made a comparative study of spills in China and in Việt Nam by cross referencing material from his reading with his own observations:

清異錄云:夜有急、苦作燈之緩。批杉染硫黃待用、遇火即焰呼爲「引光奴」、後遂有貨者、易名「火寸」。 In the *Qingyilu* [Records of Pure

140 *Bamboo iconography*

Figure 8.8 **"Đình đuốc"** (bamboo torch – *used during sacrifices*). Oger, 1909, p. 87.

Marvels], by Tao Gu 陶穀 (?-970) in the Song dynasty, "at night time when there is an emergency one may waste time by trying to light a lamp. Usually one uses a strip of purslane stalk covered with sulphur. It catches fire immediately, the flame being called the "slave who leads to the light". Later traders replaced this expression "small fire (huo cun 火寸)". 今本國人用竹薄片浸晒染硫黃亦類是製 俗呼爲炻焰 Nowadays the people of our country [*i.e.* Việt Nam. T.N.] use a slip of bamboo coated with sulphur. The production method is similar to the previous example and bears the name "đóm diêm 炻焰 (match) in the vernacular".[2]

Figure 8.11 requires some explanations. It describes a strategy used by bandits to find out where money has been hidden. But here, the torturer, who is holding the torch, is too well dressed to be a felon, wearing a turban around his hair, a fitted tunic tied at the side with a belt with wide ends (different to the belts around the tunics worn by women). The victim, crouching on the ground, has his hands tied behind his back with his head sticking out of a tear in the "basket-ware boat (thuyền nan)". The fire is lit at the edge of the basket, which burns all around the victim's head, not touching him but getting closer and closer. This illustration is perhaps showing torture to make a robber confess to where he has hidden the booty.

Use of split bamboo cut into lengths 141

Figure 8.9 **"Cắm ống đóm"** (replacing a bamboo spill in a container). Oger, 1909, p. 156.

One does not need to be reminded that torture depends on the psychological effect it has. Here, it is hoped that fear will extract either a confession or money. Some famous bandits used even simpler methods with prompt results: they placed husks of paddy rice ("vỏ trấu") under the victim's eyelid. As he writhed in pain, he begged his family to deliver the ransom, with the desired result achieved.

Figure 8.12 shows an artisan making *ex-votos*: he is gluing paper over a framework in the shape of a horse. The man (or woman) is dressed in loose garments, as the work is not physically demanding. Like certain other corporations, these artisans had clearly signalled shop fronts. Shops in Hà Nội, on "*Ex-voto* Street (phố Hàng Mã)" – not a particularly big street but well stocked – offered all sorts of votive objects with bamboo frames covered in paper that were the expression of life after death; more than the living, the dead require not only objects of everyday life but also all they had been deprived of during their life. A paper concubine or a big house, an expensive car or gold bars, luxury clothing were all well received. A concession to modern-day economics, the banknotes are in large enough denominations to defy bankruptcy. Other votive objects are made to serve as mounts for various divinities – horses (or elephants) with their harness but without a rider – to be burned for the gods and goddesses and even for the protective spirits of national

142 *Bamboo iconography*

Figure 8.10 Double bamboo container for tooth picks and spills fixed to a wooden partition. Hòa Bình Province. 1989. Photograph by Đinh Trọng Hiếu.

or local historiography (the "Two Sisters", or "Dame Triệu Âu", for example). The demand for these votive objects is such that, nowadays, certain villages specialize in making the frameworks, which are then sent to workshops in the suburbs of the capital to be decorated and sold there. The same artisans also make paper toys (with bamboo frameworks) for children for the Mid-Autumn Festival. The previous month on Wandering Souls Day (full moon of the seventh month), *ex-votos* of all sorts were burned.[3]

Figure 8.13 shows a dancer dressed in urban fashion tapping two lengths of bamboo together as clappers. They provide a rhythmic accompaniment to a song. This is one of the musical instruments in learned music or "chamber music". Used

Figure 8.11 **"Đốt quanh tra tiền"** (being burned all around [the neck] to admit where money has been hidden). Oger, 1909, p. 205.

in the same way, clappers are played to accompany dancers who are also trained to sing and play while they perform.

The percussion instrument in Figure 8.14 provides the rhythm for songs in the "ca trù" tradition (Anisensel, 2012), a vocal style accompanied on string instruments. Also called "phách" or "sinh" (clappers), it consists of a length of split bamboo

144   *Bamboo iconography*

Figure 8.12 Maker of *ex-votos* (authors' title). Oger, 1909, p. 69.

Figure 8.13 "*Kĩ nữ kích sách dĩ ca*" (a dancer playing two bamboo sticks [clappers] to accompany a song). Oger, 1909, p. 24.

Use of split bamboo cut into lengths 145

Figure 8.14 **"Nhà trò đánh phách"** (professional percussionist playing bamboo instruments as accompaniment to songs). Oger, 1909, p. 285.

Figure 8.15 **"Bán sực tắc"** (advertising in the street with clappers). Oger, 1909, p. 95.

146 *Bamboo iconography*

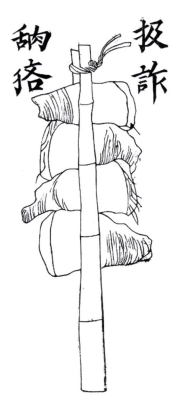

Figure 8.16 **"Kẹp chả thịt lợn"** (clip for grilling pork). Oger, 1909, p. 529.

placed on the ground (or on a mat), played with two (or three, if double sticks are used) wooden sticks. In "ca trù", a professional percussionist plays this instrument to begin the performance and then provides the rhythm as the song progresses. This instrument is also part of the blind musicians travelling orchestra ("hát xẩm").

To announce his arrival and to attract the attention of his customers, the Chinese noodle seller (or his assistant) uses bamboo clappers, which, although they are very small (the sound box can be held in the palm of the hand), can make a deafening noise (see Figure 8.15). The two notes produced by the instrument are an onomatopoeia for the type of soup that is for sale: "sực/tắc". Present in towns both in the north and in the south, the street seller sets down his heavy boxes, one containing a big pan of broth on a stove and the other, a stand with noodles and various ingredients. Playing the clappers, the assistant goes around the narrow streets in the area informing the inhabitants and taking their orders, which he immediately passes on to the noodle seller. Organized in this way, the noodle seller can attract his customers while maintaining his mobility, whereas the "phở" street seller, without the advantages of this noisy advertising, tends eventually to become sedentary.

Use of split bamboo cut into lengths 147

Figure 8.17 **"Bán tôm"** (selling [skewer] prawns). Oger, 1909, p. 698.

A thin piece of bamboo is split lengthwise at one end (see Figure 8.16). Chunks of seasoned pork are placed in the split part and then the open ends are tied together securely with a fine "bamboo strip (dây lạt)", and the resulting parcel is placed on hot coals. The fire is fanned constantly. The meat sizzles and has cooked before the strip has time to burn through. A delicious aroma fills the air. Street sellers prepare two sorts of meat this way: one is sliced, seasoned pork "simple grilled pork (chả thịt lợn)"; the other is made with "minced pork" and various other ingredients ("chả viên"). Both types of grilled pork are served with cold rice "angels' hair" noodles with a "nước mắm"-based sauce with some sugar, lemon juice, chilli and garlic. In the tales of "trạng Quỳnh (laureate Quỳnh)",[4] a scholar, who never had enough money but always plenty of ideas, used to eat his dull, plain rice standing near grilling

148 *Bamboo iconography*

Figure 8.18 **Xóc cua** (Crabs placed on pins). Dumoutier, 1908, p. 141.

meat to enjoy the aroma. When the seller demanded to be paid for the benefit of the aroma, he gave her a coin. As soon as she hid it in her tunic, the crafty scholar took it back with a sleight-of-hand, calling out: "I ate the aroma of the grilled meat, so I'm paying with the aroma of my money (Ăn hơi chả, trả hơi tiền)". The madman in Rabelais (*Third Book*) pays for the delicious smell of roast by jingling his money.

The similarity with the method for grilling pork is misleading (see Figure 8.17). The prawns on this skewer are not prepared for cooking but for drying. These are good sized, as three of them fill one bamboo skewer. Contact with metal instruments of any kind is precluded to avoid the undesirable flavour of "tanh" (smell of cold fish). So, bamboo skewers are a very good choice.

In Figure 8.18, the large prawns are threaded on to skewers called "xóc" (securing pin) for drying on wide, flat baskets where they are turned over from time to time, three by three, therefore saving time. They are presented for sale, still three per skewer, on the market stall.

This illustration is taken from *Essais sur les Tonkinois:*

> The paddy fields also provide food for shrimps and crabs. Crab is usually disregarded by the fishermen; only poor people bother to collect them and take them to market, having fixed them on pairs of bamboo pins ("xóc cua"): a skewer of five crabs costs 8 to 10 cash.[5]

The engraving provides a wealth of interesting detail. A young peasant girl wearing a turban as dishevelled as her dress is hurrying to get the freshly fished crabs onto the pins. She is finishing one basket before starting on the second basket, which she has not had time to take off her shoulder. Her round, basket-shaped hat

Use of split bamboo cut into lengths 149

Figure 8.19 "**Chẻ răng lược bí**" (splitting bamboo to make a fine-tooth comb). Oger, 1909, p. 133.

lies on the ground at her side. With her right foot resting on the pins, she carefully slides the crabs one by one into the space between the bamboo pins, tying each one in place with a fine strip of bamboo; held this way, although their legs and claws are free to move, the crabs can neither escape nor pinch. Three of these pairs of pins have already been prepared. The goods in the basket in the foreground are not identifiable.

Crab is prepared with great care. The shell is removed and then set aside with the body and the legs while the "tomalley (gạch cua)" is reserved in a bowl. Then, the claws and the body are crushed in a mortar, the resulting paste is sieved through a cloth to remove any pieces of shell and the liquid is collected in a bowl. All the ingredients are cooked in broth with vegetables to be used as a sauce for vermicelli: this is the delicious "bún riêu cua", which can only be found in restaurants in Việt Nam and is never served elsewhere in the world.

150 *Bamboo iconography*

Figure 8.20 A comb (untitled). Oger, 1909, p. 241.

Figure 8.21 "**Cái rọ**" (accessory for picking fruit). Oger, 1909, p. 408.

In the foreground, a woman, dressed in urban style and wearing a turban, is sitting crouched over her chopping block cutting up bamboo (from the stronger, cortical part of the trunk) into sections (see Figure 8.19). She will then use a finer knife to split the length of bamboo up to a certain point to make the "teeth of the comb (răng lược)". The following illustration shows a finished, fine comb ("lược bí") with decoration, used to remove headlice. In the background, combs made in this way are displayed in a basket ready for sale.

Figure 8.21 is either incomplete or unclear. It shows the upper part of a tool for picking fruit from high branches. At one end, a bamboo trunk is split at intervals into sections about 20 centimetres deep. These "teeth" are then held apart by a ring

Use of split bamboo cut into lengths 151

of weaving about 10 centimetres from the top (distance not respected in this drawing). The "teeth" made this way can be slipped between the fruit-bearing branches to detach the fruit.

The fruit then falls into the bamboo receptacle without being damaged. This is a cheap, simple and efficient tool, especially if it were to have a longer handle.

The tool depicted in this illustration is a long, upside-down pole; the bamboo trunk is used with its base towards the top. The lower part with a short side shoot is raised in the air and used as a hook. In the drawing, the man is using the

Figure 8.22 **"Bẻ khế"** (picking carambola). Oger, 1909, p. 158.

152 *Bamboo iconography*

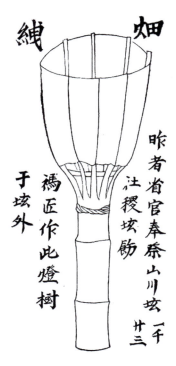

Figure 8.23 **"Đèn giấy"** (paper lampshade). (In past times, when a provincial mandarin official carried out a sacrifice to the spirits of the mountains, the rivers, the earth and the harvests, artisans who made votive objects in paper were ordered to produce lamps to be placed around the sacrificial esplanade.) Oger, 1909, p. 504.

hook to catch hold of fruit to make it fall. This tool is more efficient and easier to make than the accessory on the previous page but does not protect the fruit from damage when it falls. The carambola (or star fruit) harvested in this way may not be in perfect condition on the market stall. However, for immediate consumption at home, for instance as additional flavouring in a broth, it doesn't really matter.

This lampshade is made in a similar way to the fruit picker (see Figure 8.22) but with improvements according to the requirements of the solemn circumstances.

At intervals around one end, a thick length of bamboo is split into "teeth" to a depth of 20 to 30 centimetres, according to the desired size of the object. A cord made of bamboo strips is carefully wound around the base of the "teeth" so that they do not split further; then, the teeth are separated out by weaving lengths of fine bamboo to-and-fro at the base and also higher up, so that the lampshade appears to open out gracefully, like a flower. A holder for an oil lamp or a candle is placed inside the resulting framework then paper is glued on the outside.

Use of split bamboo cut into lengths 153

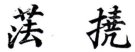

Figure 8.24 "**Nạo mướp**" (tool for peeling [and not grating] cucurbits). Oger, 1909, p. 191.

Although this tool seems to be quite insignificant, it is, in fact, very useful for peeling fruit and vegetables. How does it work? The enlarged drawing shows a square-ended knife ("dao bài") and a small bamboo element. The latter is used to block the blade. The knife is placed on it according to the thickness of peel to be removed and the fruit or vegetable to be peeled is then rubbed against it. The square-ended knife, with its notoriously razor-sharp blade, can then remove the required thickness of peel from all over the vegetable or fruit.

Notes

1 On the dykes, cf. *supra*, chapter 5, pp. 74–75
2 *VĐLN*, q. IX, f° 7b-8a.
3 See https://thanhnien.vn/doi-song/tet-giap-ngo-ngua-giay-bac-trieu-dat-hang-396436. html [Accessed: 21/03/2020].
4 "Trạng" is an abbreviation of "Trạng nguyên 狀元", title of the top laureate (or first place in the class of doctors) at the higher examinations at the palace.
5 Dumoutier, 1908, p. 141, figure 47.

9 Basket-making

Figure 9.1 depicts the first steps in making a basket. The bamboo has been felled and then cut up into slats, cut into fine strips, ready to be woven. According to the size and the density of the weave, a wide variety of utensils can be made with these materials. There are "standardized" models, even though basket-making remains a craft and the production is sold at market; for example, a "stand for a cooking pot (cái rế)" will be different according to the size of the utensil. The weaver will always be careful to respect the dimensions required or the product may not find a buyer. Sometimes, however, for use for a particular purpose by a particular individual in a private household, a basket may be made at home on a "one off" basis. As bamboo is widely distributed and grows in private gardens, pieces such as these may be perfectly adequate for the intended use and may also be of great practical and artistic value.

It should be noted that, in general, basket-weaving is done in a crouching position or sitting on the ground.

Bamboo is not only used by basket makers but also by artisans who make *ex-votos*. In this case, it is used for the framework, as is the case of this dryer for paper to be used for decoration, as shown in Figure 9.2.

On a low framework made of bamboo trunks, two cylindrical elements have been installed. They are made of wide slats with sticks inserted in the weave of the top part.

The paper has been coloured. It is damp and has been hung on a baton so that it can dry; this is the case for the cylinder in the foreground, where all the batons are in use. The illustrator has seen the point of leaving the cylinder in the background empty so that the reader can see how the system works.

Two positions for working are shown in Figure 9.3: the older of the two artisans is seated on a low, wooden platform "tearing a strip of bamboo (tước lạt tre)" held between his front teeth. The other, younger artisan has one knee raised, with one foot on the chair, is splitting bamboo or "smoothing a slat (vót thanh tre)", most certainly for making picture frames. Several pieces of trapeze-shaped furniture are shown here, but the most surprising of them are the frames that appear to be miraculously levitating. Intentional gaucherie? A different conception of (inadequate?) space.

DOI: 10.4324/9781003350347-12

Basket-making 155

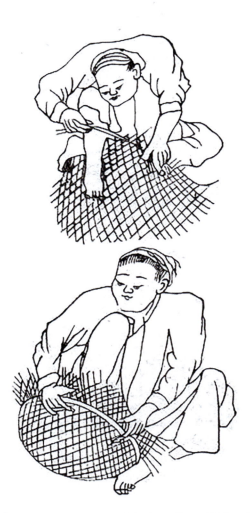

Figure 9.1 **"Đan rổ"** (weaving an open-work basket). Oger, 1909, p. 364.

156 *Bamboo iconography*

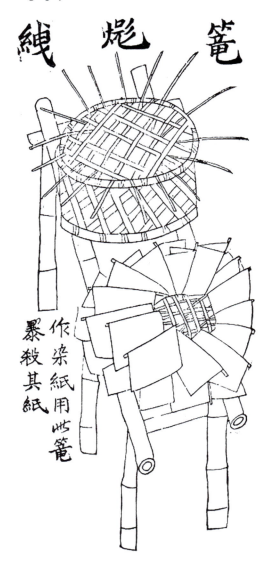

Figure 9.2 **"Lồng phơi giấy"** (dryer for paper). (When dyed paper is made, it is dried in this way.) Oger, 1909, p. 537.

Although the title is erroneous (see Figure 9.4), this illustration has been included here for its mistaken use of the word "bamboo". The fan being woven is not made from bamboo (one is included on the next page) but from a palm leaf: the clearly visible veins of the leaf give this woven fan its shape and are used to weave with strips of leaf taken from the plant. The resulting fan is clearly depicted above the artisan's head. There are several sorts of fan for different uses: elegant

Basket-making 157

Figure 9.3 (No title: other bamboo craftsmen). Oger, 1909, p. 32.

Figure 9.4 **"Đan quạt tre"** (weaving a bamboo fan). Title error. Oger, 1909, p. 150.

158   *Bamboo iconography*

Figure 9.5 **"Làm quạt giấy"**. Dumoutier, 1908, p. 66.

fans made of palm leaves that do not fold up; simpler, commonplace fans in spongy bamboo fibre "quạt vĩ" or "quạt nan" (see Figure 9.19); foldable fans with a bamboo framework, the open position giving the object its name, covered with paper or fabric as shown in the next illustration.

This drawing, taken from *Essais sur les Tonkinois*, shows another craft that uses a bamboo framework: making "paper fans (quạt giấy)".[1]

> The bamboo, cut into equal lengths, is split into thin blades and then sold in that state to fan-makers. These craftsmen choose the blades, and gather twenty together and fix them at one end with copper wire, the ends of which are riveted to rings of the same metal. The blades are then held together upright and the ends rounded off with a file, and each blade is carefully worked, softened and sanded. That is the end of the man's role. The fan frame is then passed to the women to cover the fans with paper. [. . .] The paper is very thin; even paper from old books is used for making cheap fans, this paper being strengthened by a coat of fermented wild persimmon juice

Basket-making 159

called *quả-cài*[2] Annam. This liquid is very important in various industries in China and is found on English markets under the name of *Oil of Persimmon (in English in the original)* and costs, in Chang-hai, about 34 francs for 100 kilos. [. . .] So a layer of persimmon juice is spread on the papers with a small flat brush made of pine needles. The paper is then cut using a pattern and stuck to each side of the fan frame with persimmon juice. This liquid is sufficiently sticky to act as glue: it sticks the two sheets of paper together indissolubly and produces a sort of parchment finish, because these fans do not tear easily at the folds. When complete, the fans made of ordinary paper are put in bundles of ten and sold for one ligature of cash per bundle; the more inferior sort are sold for only six hundred for ten. The inhabitants of Kẻ-vác, in Thượng-linh prefecture, make a special type of fan using paper coloured with indigo and covered with motifs and open- work arabesques, creating a sort of lace.[3]

The social role of the fan

Following his explanations for making fans, Dumoutier then discusses the "social role of the fan":

Everyone's vade-mecum in Annam, whatever the social class, the fan takes of place among all the accessories of everyday life in Indochina, along with betel quid. In Europe, the exclusive role of the fan is fashion accessory, aesthetic object or ladies' jewel. Here it is an object of necessity, to be found in the hands of the agricultural labourer, the marching soldier or sentinel, the carrier in town or the solemn mandarin official: of course this does not prevent the young girls or ladies of Annam from playing with this "State machine", as J. Janin called it, as knowingly, even as gracefully, as any elegant of Puerta del Sol. But here people are poor; the sumptuary and inquisitorial laws under which they have been obliged to suppress their artistic aspiration for so long have prevented the decoration of the fan, such as is seen in China and Japan, with delicate painting upon fine costly fabrics, valuable lacquer and intricate ivory figures. The fan with mobile blades is sometimes made in horn or more rarely in ivory: but these are objects that one finds only on exceptional occasions and are therefore of little ethnographical interest. It is the bamboo fan that reigns sovereign in the (Tonkin) country.". "During the traditional betrothal ceremony, it is always the done thing for the future bride to hide herself. Sorcerers sell magic fans with spells written between the papers. Fanning someone

160 *Bamboo iconography*

> with such a fan and all manner of disasters may befall him or his family. But the fan is not only used for curses. A fan addressed to a young girl with no further explanation is a tender declaration, to which she is seen to react favourably if she keeps it. Also the fan is the best solution Annam people have found so far as protection from rabid dogs. They say that a wild fearless dog will run away like a hen once it feels the breath of cool air sent from a fan waved in front of its nose.[4]
>
> In complete agreement with Dumoutier's remarks, it should also be noted that, in the case of kidnapping of girls and/or children, "mẹ mìn" (witches) used fans coated with soporific or anaesthetising products, fanning a child in the face with such a fan and he/she would follow the "witch" in a docile manner. The fan remains an indispensable accessory for the medium (masculine or feminine) during ritual trance sessions: whether the medium takes alcohol or spits out saliva after chewing betel quid, he/she or an assistant will cover their mouth with a beautiful fan, either through shyness or coquetry. Even nowadays during a traditional betrothal ceremony, it is still considered the "done" thing for the future bride to hide behind a fan. Having such an important social role, it is not surprising that, in the time of the emperors, a costly fan figured among the most valued gifts that a sovereign could bestow upon a deserving subject.[5]

The weaving of the boat shown in Figure 9.6 is strangely similar to that of a basket or a rack – because the work is, in fact, the same in terms of bamboo basket-making. The bamboo trunk has been cut and split into thin strips of different widths because the interweave for a boat is larger than for a basket. The same procedure is followed as for a basket, especially as the boat here is an "oval woven boat (thuyền nan)". The sides are reinforced, as on a basket, by circling with a band of larger, stronger, good-quality bamboo (cortical bamboo, or "tre cật"). When the boat is complete, it can be coated with tar or lacquer to make it watertight. However, a bailer or scoop is always at hand to lighten the vessel if water should leak in. There are woven boats in other shapes: oval, large, large round ("thuyền thúng"), small round ("thuyền mủng").

In Figure 9.7, it would be more precise to call the chicken coop "bu gà" (without a base), rather than "lồng gà" (with a base). The artisan is using lengths of bamboo that have been split into fairly thick slats of mediocre quality (the spongy part of the bamboo trunk, "ruột tre") because hens are not strong enough to break the cage. The part that requires better-quality bamboo is the opening of the cage, which is reinforced with a plaited weave or by using the cortical layer of the bamboo.

The weaving in Figure 9.8 is the same as in Figure 9.6, but here, the piece is much bigger and requires up to three weaver women sitting on it while they work.

Basket-making 161

Figure 9.6 **"Đan thuyền"** (weaving [the hull of] a boat). Oger, 1909, p. 260.

It is not clear to what use this will be put: a big boat-basket or a "rack (phên)"? At the stage shown here, the basket is not rigid yet. It could be stiffened and strengthened by fixing it to bamboo trunks slit in half, lengthwise, and attached firmly to the basket with straps. In that case, it would become a "partition (liếp)".

Weaving with wire is only of interest here if the shape of the tray cover imitates bamboo basketwork (see Figure 9.9). Indeed, the framework, particularly the rim, must be in bamboo slats (whereas the rest of the frame must be in wood because it is not possible to work bamboo into a flat and curvy shape such as shown here). In earlier times, tray covers where made entirely from bamboo. Nowadays, fine, carefully "smoothed (vót, chuốt)" bamboo stems are used once again to revive the old tradition of making high-quality covers for use at table to protect delicacies that are ready to eat.

162 Bamboo iconography

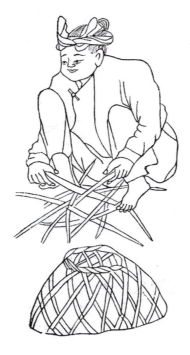

Figure 9.7 **"Đan lồng gà"** (weaving a chicken coop). Oger, 1909, p. 272.

Figure 9.8 **"Đan phên"** (weaving a partition or a rack). Oger, 1909, p. 39.

Basket-making 163

Figure 9.9 **"Đan lồng bàn [dây] thép"** (weaving a tray cover (with wire). Oger, 1909, p. 362.

Craftsmen are perpetuating the production of various sorts of cages (for birds or crickets, for example) still using bamboo. Such goods are sold for high prices to aficionados.

From Figure 9.10 onwards, the various uses of bamboo basket ware will be documented. A peasant girl (recognizable from her tucked up skirt) is gathering these floating aquatic plants ("bèo cái ", *Pistia stratiotes L*.) into her basket using two bamboo poles tied together to form a cross. The basket is the "wide open weave basket (rổ lớn)" type. A "rổ" is an open-weave basket for edible goods (water plants, vegetables) that allows water to drain through, unlike the "rá (closely woven basket)" that retains contents such as rice or cowpea seed. These "rá" are usually made in standard sizes because the user should be able to estimate the volume of contents at a glance, whereas there are several sizes of "rổ".

Figure 9.11 is another use for "rổ", where the open weave allows water to drip through. This peasant woman is caring for her young cabbage plants, gently

164 *Bamboo iconography*

Figure 9.10 **"Vớt bèo"** (collecting water cabbage). Oger, 1909, p. 194.

sprinkling them with water without damaging them. She is not using a metal watering can – unknown to farmers until the beginning of the 20th century – but a "rổ", which sprinkles droplets just as well and also has other uses.

A large example of the "oval boat in bamboo basket work (thuyền nan)" used as a ferry boat is shown in Figure 9.12. So, it is fitted differently to similar simple craft: the woman rower, a strong peasant lady, is standing on a deck made of boards with her oar tied to the boat. She is rowing standing up and acts as counterweight

Basket-making 165

Figure 9.11 **"Tưới rau cải"** (watering cabbages). Oger, 1909, p. 584.

to her passengers (not portrayed here), who sit on the cross bar towards the prow of the boat. The oar is used to propel the boat and also to steer it, when necessary. From where she is standing, the boat woman can move forwards a little – or back – to stabilize the boat. There is sometimes a small scoop in the boat, used by one of the passengers to empty out any water that may seep in or wash over the rim; this will lighten the load. Operated skilfully, the boat can easily ferry passengers across rivers, unless the water is very rough due to bad weather. The boat can go forwards, stop, turn or go backwards, sailing in all directions.

Boats made of woven bamboo slats are often called "basket-boats (thuyền thúng)", whatever the shape or size. But the true "basket-boat" is round in shape. Another name takes into account the shape and the size: "thuyền mủng (small oval boat)".

166 *Bamboo iconography*

Figure 9.12 **"Đò ngang"** (boat for crossing a river).[6] Oger, 1909, p. 115.

In Figure 9.13, the medium-sized basket-ware boat ("thuyền nan"), has three crosspieces for consolidation, fixed a little below the rim, which can also be used as seating; the hull is often wet. One of the passengers is sitting on a crosspiece, propelling the boat with a pole – a sign that the boat is sailing on a shallow lake – otherwise an oar would be used. They are collecting lotus flowers, and lotus grows in the muddy floor of shallow stretches of water. A vessel such as this easily carries two people and their harvest.

Figure 9.14 is a similar vessel, but smaller, the same size as the peasant carrying it. It is called "thuyền thúng" in reference to the weaving technique, similar to that of a basket, even though the vessel is oval. It has three crosspieces used for a maximum of two passengers sitting face to face. Smaller boats of the same design do not have crosspieces, but they remain efficient and manageable.

Figure 9.13 **"Hái hoa sen"** (collecting lotus flowers [in a woven boat]). Oger, 1909, p. 230.

One of the authors of this work, Đinh Trọng Hiếu, at the age of eight, was on a boat like this with his mother; they were caught in a whirlpool and managed to escape from it by rowing energetically. This happened when the dykes broke at Vĩnh Yên during the flooding from July to November in 1945. They were both rowers, and while one of them was using the oar, the other was bailing.

To stay dry in a little boat without a crosspiece as a seat, then one crouches.

The model shown in Figure 9.15 is the true "basket-boat (thuyền thúng)", in the shape of a truly circular basket (rather than oval). This small model is not strengthened with a crosspiece, but the consolidating rim of the vessel is clearly visible. Because of its shape and the limitation for use by one person only, the boat is subject to the same pressure from the water all over its surface and therefore remains very stable as long as the hull has been carefully caulked. There are many substances such as plant sap, animal substances (faeces of cattle or buffalo were

Figure 9.14 **"Đội cái thuyền thúng"** (carrying a basket-boat [over the head]). Oger, 1909, p. 43.

used in the past), tar or lacquer (an expensive product) for "caulking (sàm thuyền)". A small, well-caulked boat can have a fairly dry floor, particularly if it is easy to steer, riding the crest of waves in a surprising way. One pair of short oars is sufficient to manage this little masterpiece of design. Sometimes, two ordinary oars are fixed to the sides and can be rowed alternately by the two legs of an invisible person lying on the bottom of the vessel. Sometimes, one oar is enough. On this drawing, the rower is sitting on the bottom of the boat.

Another sort of oar that is rare (see Figure 9.16). This is rather a complex construction. The blade of the oar is made in basketwork, strengthened around the edges and joined by a bird's foot-shaped bamboo framework to a bamboo pole. The type of boat for which this oar would be used is unclear, as are any particular advantages of the design.

With the correct weave and with the use of very fine, flat strips of bamboo, a "flake" (a small bamboo trellis), in Figure 9.17 called a "vỉ", remains pliable, unlike other "flakes" that are thicker, stiffer or that can only be rolled up one way ("phên" ou "cót"). Shown here is a thin, flexible flake for rolling up cooked rice in order to press it. This crushes the grains of rice and makes them into a sort of soft paste. The paste is wrapped in a cloth to prevent it from drying too fast. After a day or two, a hard crust forms on the surface, keeping the inside damp. The rice paste made this way is called "cơm nắm" or "cơm vắt" ("rice pressed with the fist", or "squeezed rice"); it can be kept for longer than rice prepared without this treatment. To eat the soft part, the paste loaf is cut with a knife, and the crust is removed. The

Figure 9.15 **"Bě dầm thuyền"** (boating using short, curved oars). Oger, 1909, p. 320.

inside part is delicious; it is mixed with bits of crushed, shredded pork ("thịt ruốc", or "chà bông"). It is a good food to be taken on long journeys, and from the early 20th century onwards, carried as picnic food.

The panel in Figure 9.18, woven in chevron pattern, does not have a precise purpose; that will depend on the thickness of the strips of bamboo and on the addition of crosspieces. The panel illustrated here measures a maximum of 2 metres by one and a half (although smaller panels are also available). The woven element of the panel is pliable, flexible and can even be rolled up (depending on the thickness of the strips). When it is reinforced with thick bamboo bars attached firmly with supple straps, the rack becomes rigid and can be used as a partition or a temporary door. It would need great force or sharp, heavy instruments to make a hole in such a panel and then break through the crosspieces. Panels like this one are used as

170 *Bamboo iconography*

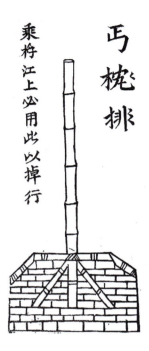

Figure 9.16 **"Cái dầm bài"** (oar). (Used on a river for rowing.) Oger, 1909, p. 448.

Figure 9.17 **"Nắm cơm"** (pressing cooked rice in a flexible bamboo flake). Oger, 1909, p. 608.

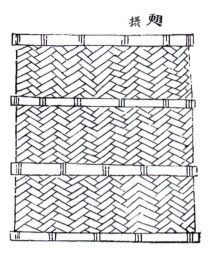

Figure 9.18 **"Cánh liếp"** (bamboo rack [for drying fruit or for use as a partition]). Oger, 1909, p. 42.

protection from sun, wind and dust, and for privacy. If a thicker panel than this were to be padded with straw, it could also be used as a shield against arrows.

The bamboo trellis fan ("quạt vĩ" or "quạt nan") in Figure 9.19 is a fan that does not fold up. Commonly used to make a draught or to fan a fire for cooking, it is a cheap version and lasts longer than a paper fan. It is closely woven with spongy strips (cut from the inside part of bamboo) so that it is slightly pliable. It is mounted on a bamboo stalk on one side (making that side rigid); held by the stalk side, with a flick of the wrist, it fans efficiently to create a breeze. Rarely used in an urban context, in a rustic setting, it has its charm.

Basket-ware can be polyvalent. The same type of weave can be shaped and used differently. Consolidated or not, a flake can be used for drying grain; consolidated with bamboo mountings, it can be used as a partition or a moveable door; rolled up and attached at the ends, it can be a bin for stocking paddy rice. In Figure 9.20, the drawing shows a "cót thóc (paddy rice silo)": a rolled-up flake, held in place with a strong rope, its base on a shallow basket ("nong" or "nia") whose circular edging holds the bin in shape (not to be confused with a possible base of the bin). This type of bin is used temporarily to stock paddy rice between different stages of conditioning: threshing, drying, then husking. Rice that has had the husk removed is stored in other receptacles (jars, chests) before and after whitening and riddling. The "granary (vựa)" is a rare institution. Where the small size of the paddy fields does not provide a large production of rice to be stocked, it is replaced by the "flake silo (cót vựa)", installed temporarily during the harvest at the producer's fields or in a more permanent manner in public stores.

According to Lê Quý Đôn in *Miscellaneous Chronicles of the Pacified Frontier*, the "cót thóc" is also used for the payment of taxes. The payment is made in measures of paddy rice and in "cót" in Thuận Hóa province (Central Việt Nam) in

172 *Bamboo iconography*

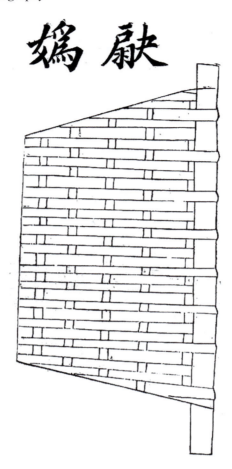

Figure 9.19 **"Quạt vỉ"** (bamboo trellis fan). Oger, 1909, p. 652.

Figure 9.20 **"Cót thóc"** (bamboo flake cylinder to hold paddy rice). Oger, 1909, p. 16.

Figure 9.21 **"Đổ thóc vào cót"** (tipping paddy rice into a rolled flake cylinder). Oger, 1909, p. 630.

the 18th century. The "cót" for paying taxes must be 3,4m[7] long and 3,2m[8] wide, as measured on the rectangle of flake, unrolled and laid flat.[9] Supposedly, the extra 22,5cms in length are to allow for the overlap at the join, when the flake is rolled around to make a cylinder so that the grains of rice cannot leak out. Also in the document quoted earlier, the "cót thóc" existed in "quarter cót (góc cót)", or a half of that, so an eighth of "cót thóc".[10] Thus, proving that a surface measurement could be used as a measure of volume.[11]

This drawing confirms the commentary on the previous illustration: the cylinder made by rolling the flake is resting on a "large winnowing basket (cái nia)" and not on the ground. This has practical advantages: the rice is not in contact with the damp or dirty floor, and the edge of the basket maintains the cylinder in shape. This rice bin has no rope halfway up the side to hold its shape, as shown in Figure 9.20, but such an addition is not always necessary, and instead, it is replaced with a "seam" joining the two edges of the flake, using bamboo ties. The farmer can tip his paddy rice into the silo without fearing that the edges will separate. A bin of this size (judging by the height of the peasant) can weigh more than one or two quintals

174   Bamboo iconography

Figure 9.22 **"Thiến chó"** (castrating a dog). Oger, 1909, p. 360.

or more. The basket containing the paddy rice to be stored is a large "thúng (a large tightly woven basket)".

This surgical operation is made possible by using a straightjacket made of bamboo flake: the dog is literally swaddled in this pliable flake, which is wound around, providing several layers, not to keep the animal warm but to prevent it moving while it is being emasculated. It should be noted that, although the flake is pliable in the direction of the roll, it is stiff in the other direction, particularly if it is rolled around several times. This is so that the dog cannot move or bite, even though the back legs are left free.

Cicatrization is encouraged by exposing the wound to the smoke produced by a plait of burning straw. So that the neutered dog does not become too docile and too

Basket-making 175

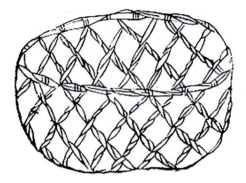

Figure 9.23 **"Sọt"** (basket/crate). Oger, 1909, p. 426.

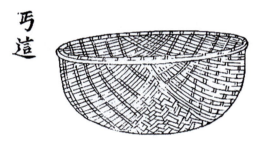

Figure 9.24 **"Cái rá"** (closely woven bamboo basket, for washing rice before cooking). Oger, 1909, p. 252.

gentle to guard the house properly, it is current practice to insert a small shard into what is left of the genitals; then, the dog will be at least as aggressive, if not more, as before it was castrated.

In Figure 9.23, the crate is made in basketwork that is not much to look at but it is extremely useful and versatile. It is woven with thin straps of bamboo and has several qualities: the crudest kind, made with inexpensive strips from the inside part of the bamboo ("lạt ruột"), is a crate for carrying large-sized fruit (melons, watermelons); to make a stronger crate, all that is necessary is to use strips cut from the stronger external part of the bamboo ("lạt cật"). These strips are plaited, and the result is surprising: the crate produced can be used to carry extremely heavy loads without ever breaking. Because of this, it was used to block the access channels for foreign ships by submerging these baskets filled with large lumps of rock and clods of earth.[12] Another similar method was also used on land – "Large square baskets in woven bamboo (竹筐 "trúc khuông") filled with earth are used to consolidate breaches in the ramparts"[13] or to fill breaches in the dykes.

176 *Bamboo iconography*

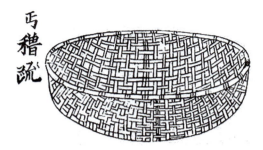

Figure 9.25 **"Cái rổ thưa"** (open weave basket) used for other goods than rice, notably for washing vegetables. Oger, 1909, p. 394.

The type of basket in Figure 9.24 is emblematic of a rice-growing civilisation. With the "rổ" (see Figure 9.25), they are always to be found in the kitchen of a rural dwelling, in their particular place, always ready to hand. The "rá" basket is about 25 centimetres in diameter, not very deep (not as deep as this drawing would imply). It is carefully made, using the cortical layer of the bamboo woven very close, letting the water flow through but not the rice. It is used exclusively for washing the rice for the family meals. Although the treatment of rice has changed considerably, washing it before cooking remains an important tradition. This removes the husks that may still be adhering to it. Enough rice for the two or three daily meals is placed in the basket, and care is taken to avoid an overflow. The basket is put in water to soak. The rice is rubbed hard against the rough bottom of the basket using a circular movement of the right hand ("vo gạo") while holding the basket carefully in place with the left hand. The water is run off carefully while the remaining husks of the rice ("vỏ trấu"), being lighter, rise to the surface of the water and are carried away. Then, the drained, wet, softened rice is carefully inspected, and any other foreign bodies such as grit or cockroach droppings are removed. It is no good preparing some tasty rice to go with a delicious dish if a nasty piece of grit gets between the teeth and spoils the whole meal!

The inseparable cousin of the previous example, the "rổ thưa" is a completely different character. Whereas the "rá" is tightly woven, the "rổ" has a wide enough weave for the water to run out easily without the vegetables falling through. It is made with crisscross bamboo strips, with different-sized gaps according to the intended use of the utensil: closer for green cowpeas, wider for leafy greens. All the strips are held in place by the top-quality bamboo edging; the durability and strength of a "rá" or a "rổ" depends on a good rim – making one is called "cạp rổ, cạp rá". These utensils are made to last; they are not thrown away when they are worn out but, if possible, they are repaired. A saying arises from this custom that describes a certain type of partnership: a widower who marries a widow getting together as a new couple. They are described as "rổ rá cạp lại", or as utensils that have been restored and are still serviceable.

For conditioning rice, many different utensils are available to the Vietnamese farmer; they have various names and various uses. Here, the woman is using a

Basket-making 177

Figure 9.26 "**Sẩy thóc lép**" (winnowing [rice chaff] or hollow paddy rice). Oger, 1909, p. 659.

"winnowing basket" to remove chaff from the rice. She puts some rice in this "wide flat closely woven basket (cái nia)" to "winnow (sẩy)", a task that is different from that using a "winnowing basket (cái quạt thóc)" intended for separating straw from the paddy rice. Bending over the basket, she flicks the rice up in the air, with a slight backward movement of the "nia", so that the chaff, which is lighter, falls out at the front but her rice is retained. This task comes after separating the milled rice from the broken rice, called "riddling (sàng)", where another loose-weave "winnowing basket", to separate rice grains from the "broken rice (tấm)", is used. Then, the broken rice is sieved with a third "winnowing basket" with an even closer weave to separate the broken rice from the "bran (cám)", a task called "winnowing to separate the bran (giần)". The two baskets for "giần" and "sàng" are similar (see Figure 9.31). There are two sorts of "hollow paddy rice (thóc lép)": "half hollow (thóc lép lửng)", and "completely hollow (thóc lép hoàn toàn)".

When there is no reference to scale in the drawings, it is not easy to distinguish between a "wide flat closely woven basket (cái nia)" for winnowing and its larger twin (that cannot be carried by one person), called "nong", which is used for drying all sorts of foodstuffs. Rather than drying things spread out on the threshing floor of a dwelling, drying in a "nong" means that, in the case of a sudden storm, it is possible to bring them inside quickly. If one compares the two drawings, (Figures 9.27

178 *Bamboo iconography*

Figure 9.27 **"Cái nia"** (medium-sized, wide, flat basket [used mainly for drying foodstuffs]). Oger, 1909, p. 117.

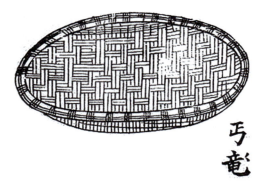

Figure 9.28 **"Cái nong"** (large, wide, flat basket for drying). Oger, 1909, p. 383.

and 9.28), the differences are obvious, particularly the greater depth of the "nong". In fact, these disparities are somewhat random, as there are "nong" that are more or less deep and also ones that are almost flat. The distinguishing feature of these two baskets is really their size. No one can carry a "nong" alone. Carrying a "nong" is always a shared task (see Figure 9.30).

The diameter of this type of basket is about the same size as the height of the average peasant and large enough for two people to lie down curled up in it, facing each other. So, in a cruel joke at the expense of hunchbacks, a folk song mocks them: "Chồng cong mà lấy vợ còng/Nằm chiếu thì chật, nằm nong thì vừa (A hunchback husband takes a stooped wife/They would be crowded on a mat, but in a 'nong', it would be roomy)". Q.E.D. In practical terms, the difference is expressed as follows: one person can hold a "nia", whereas the diameter of a "nong" is more than the span of outstretched arms.

Lê Quý Đôn noticed a similarity:

Sancai tuhui 三才圖會 [in fact *Nongshu* 農書 by Wang Zhen 王禎 (1271–1368), XV. T.N.] states that a "shai pan" 曬槃 is a woven bamboo tray for drying grain in the sun. It can be about five foot ("chi" 尺) wide. The edge

Basket-making 179

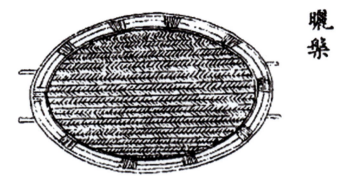

Figure 9.29 "Shaipan"[14] (tray for drying in the sun).

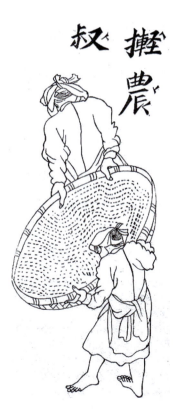

Figure 9.30 **"Khiêng nong thóc"** (two people carrying a large, flat basket for drying paddy rice). Oger, 1909, p. 525.

Figure 9.31 "**Người giần gạo**" (riddling rice). Oger, 1909, p. 248.

is slightly raised, being about five inches ("cun" 寸) deep. In the middle it is big, wide, long and flat. Two bamboo rods are placed underneath it with the ends protruding, allowing fist size handles to raise and move the basket with ease. When the weather is fine, grain is spread on it to dry it properly, [quotation from Lê Quý Đôn's comment:] when examining its shape it is the exact equivalent of what we call "bình đầu ki" 平頭箕 [or "nong". T.N.] in our country [Việt Nam. T.N.].[15]

Unless one has very long arms, it is not possible for one person to carry a "nong (large flat basket)" at arm's length. A "nong" is a closely woven bamboo basket strengthened with a thick edging made from the cortical layer of the plant. This border prevents the basket from buckling under the weight of its load and spilling the precious grains on the ground.

In a rice-growing culture, the work to condition the crop is mostly done by women, to such an extent that "giần sàng (riddling) rice to separate the bran and the broken rice)" has become the symbol of the work of a good rural housewife.

The open-weave basket for "riddling rice (sàng gạo)" (Figure 9.32); in other words, for separating the whole grains from the broken ones or for drying foodstuffs that are larger than the spaces in the weave, such as here for areca nuts. Fresh nuts are preferable for chewing if used directly after harvesting. They can be dried to preserve them or for selling at market, as here in a "sàng" basket. They are prepared using a very sharp "areca knife (dao cau)", used to cut each nut vertically into four portions

Basket-making 181

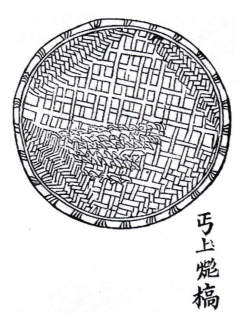

Figure 9.32 **"Cái sàng phơi cau"** (riddle for drying areca nuts). Oger, 1909, p. 382.

Figure 9.33 **"Shai gu guai"**[16] (bamboo grain riddle).

182 *Bamboo iconography*

that are then laid out to dry in the sun. An areca nut is about the size of a bantam hen's egg, so a quarter nut will not fall through the holes of this type of basket.

Two types of bamboo basket that are very similar in shape and use, the "giần" and the "sàng", which can be translated into English as "riddle" or "sieve", are intended to sort produce according to grain size. This activity can equally well be called "giần gạo" or "sàng gạo" (riddling or sieving rice to separate whole rice from broken rice or to sort the grains according to size, i.e. calibration of the grains). For finer and more homogenous products, this activity is called "rây": "rây bột", "rây đường" (sieving flour, sugar). Here, the areca nuts are only being dried, the term "sàng" being used by extension, even though the open weave basket used here is neither for sieving nor for riddling.

Lê Quý Đôn noticed another similarity here: "There is still the 'shai gu[guai]' 篩穀[筣] the term in the vernacular today in our country [Vietnam. AN] is 'sàng 床'".[17]

Figure 9.34 **"Sàng cám"** (sieving bran). Oger, 1909, p. 158.

The activities of riddling rice or sieving bran are so similar and the baskets used are so alike that the words for the task are sometimes used interchangeably; however, the use of each basket depends on the different size of the holes produced by the closeness of its weave. Bran must be removed from the rice before eating; otherwise, it is difficult to digest. Also, bran gives the rice a reddish-brown colour, which is considered a disadvantage because, for the Vietnamese, their representation of the ideal rice is that it should be very white. The bran that has been removed is collected in a "nia" and is used to fatten the pigs.

By extension, any riddling process, even for coal fragments and dust, is described using the word "giần". The only difference with rice riddling is the size of the spaces in the basket weave. The coal dust is collected in the same way as rice bran – on a "nia". The dust is then mixed with other elements (mud is one of these) to be made into pellets of fuel that will burn more slowly and is therefore more economical. This coal ersatz is not used for the forge; larger remnants of

Figure 9.35 **"Giần than làm than rèn"** (riddling coal to make fuel for the forge). Oger, 1909, p. 257.

184   *Bamboo iconography*

Figure 9.36 **"Sàng đường cát"** (sieving granulated sugar). (Sugar is extracted from the molasses produced by crushing sugar cane; women do the job of separating the smallest crystals from the rest; the larger crystals are put aside and broken down again. This explains the vernacular expression 'making granulated sugar' **chế đường cát**). Oger, 1909, p. 199.

anthracite are preferred, as they produce more heat, especially when bellows are used to activate the fire.

Same position as the foregoing for the woman at work using the same gestures: crouching or sitting on the ground she is holding a sieve about the same size as in the previous example (the one for sugar is the smallest of these), using a circular gesture to sieve the sugar. The sugar falls into a wide, flat basket ("nong"). As the work shown here is the production of granulated sugar, the text in Chinese tells us that the larger crystals remaining in the sieve will be crushed again before being sieved a second time, and so on. Sometimes, the larger pieces are sold as they are, as molasses or as brown sugar (when the product is good quality).

The "mẹt", a basket the size of a "nia" but flat, is not shown here. It is used to display goods spread out on it in the same way as the "thúng (deep basket for products)" that will be presented later. The container indicating the content, "buôn thúng, bán mẹt (buying goods in a deep basket, spreading them on a flat basket for selling)" is an expression meaning small businesses and the people

Basket-making 185

Figure 9.37 Untitled. Oger, 1909, p. 236.

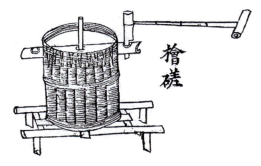

Figure 9.38 "**Cối xay**" (mill for hulling (rice). Oger, 1909, p. 247.

who run them. "Mặt mẹt" is an insult used for those whose flat features only deserve scorn.

Figure 9.37 shows an overall view of the building where the mill for hulling is worked – not to grind the rice but to break it open so that it can be separated from its chaff. To do this, the whole grains of paddy rice are poured into the mill as it turns. The surfaces that touch each other are fitted with very hard slats of male bamboo. The grains of paddy rice caught between these two surfaces burst and fall. At this point, the grains of rice and their covering (the chaff) fall into the same container. The miller is pushing a crank arm to work the active grinding disk. The crank arm is suspended from a beam to minimize the effort needed to turn it.

Figure 9.38 depicts how the grinding disks are set up on a strong bamboo base that holds the bedder firm. Above it, the upper grinder turns. An error in the drawing gives the impression that the upper disk is transparent and shows the bamboo cross piece connected to the crank arm. The operator turns the disk with a regular

186 *Bamboo iconography*

Figure 9.39 Untitled. Oger, 1909, p. 10.

Figure 9.40 "*Đảm trư*" (carrying pigs). Oger, 1909, p. 424.

movement, which ensures that the bamboo blades do not fall out, a fairly frequent occurrence that requires the always costly involvement by a specialist.

The specialist, who works all over the region, is separating the two milling disks: the bedder and the turning part. He is reinserting the slats of male bamboo on to the two contact surfaces, giving the mill a complete overhaul. In the south of Vietnam, these mills are proportionately larger and require two people to work them at the same time; the mills tended to be produced in large numbers, as described later

Figure 9.41 **"Phơi bánh đa"** (drying rice paper). Oger, 1909, p. 311.

(see Figure 10.6). However, this is now a thing of the past due to the mechanization of conditioning processes for rice for both hulling and cleaning.

In Figure 9.40, pig cages are hanging on short straps from a carrying pole with a clearly visible hook to prevent the strap from slipping. The carrier is a country farmer wearing a curiously untidy turban tied around his head.

He is wearing a tunic over short trousers. The cages are made of a very simple open-work bamboo crisscross weave, leaving wriggle room for the animals' hooves through the openings. The elongated oval shape of the cage is ingenious: the animals are restricted and cannot move around while they are being carried. The cage has a sort of lid for putting the pig into the cage, then the lid is secured with the remaining slats, but this detail is not shown here.

The drawing above shows a woman spreading rice paper wrappers on a "curved bamboo rack (phên cong)". Her hair is carefully tied, as shown by her "hen's tail (đuôi gà)", secured under her turban. She is dressed in a four-panel robe over short trousers and is standing to place the rounds of rice paper on the drying rack. The rice paper is made of rice flour and is steamed. These wrappers are called "bánh đa" or "bánh tráng". They are eaten in several different ways. They are softened by soaking in water and then used to wrap angels' hair noodles, pork (or shrimps), as well as vegetables. This is makes a "spring roll".

188   Bamboo iconography

Figure 9.42 "*Mại oa*" (frog seller). Oger, 1909, p. 222.

The same wrappers can also be used to cover various fillings to be deep-fried in oil; they are famously known as "nem" or "chả bánh đa" or "chả giò". Special rice papers with added sesame are grilled and puffed up over the fire to make a crispy nibble, eaten on its own or with dishes of raw fish ("gỏi cá"). Variations on this same rack exist as flat trays, being, in fact, more efficient for drying than the curved shape. When asked why they were using a curved rack, the rice-wrapper-makers answered that not only is a curved rack more stable as it does not buckle but is also a space saver, especially when leaned against a wall or against a trestle, as shown here. It is also more practical than a flat rack because one person is easily able to move it.

The frog basket above must be kept closed. When the animal is caught, it is slipped into the basket via an opening by the "spout" of this specially constructed basket, which is carried using a plaited bamboo shoulder strap. The seller's clothing is similar to the women's attire (a tunic with panels over short trousers). Only

Figure 9.43 **"Tát cá"** (draining a fish pond – or a paddy field – to catch the fish), left. **"Bắt ốc"** (collecting snails), right. Oger, 1909, p. 380.

the more informal style of the turban shows that this is clearly a man – and a fearsome adversary of the frogs that he catches with his bare hands.

Here are two different scenes in the same illustration. On the left, a peasant woman, recognizable from the skirt she has gathered up and tucked into her belt (she isn't wearing shorts). She is busy draining a paddy field in order to catch the fish. She is using a basin. A ceramic pot is placed next to a fish basket. Some fish are visible at the surface of the water, just behind the woman. Her skirt, tucked up before she gets into the water, can easily be let down as soon as she gets out. Where the work entails getting in and out of the water, this type of garment is far more practical than long trousers.

On the right, a young woman is wearing a turban. She is about to place a mollusc – probably a mussel – into her "snail basket (rọ ốc)". This type of basket, used interchangeably for snails, small paddy field crabs or smallish fish, is designed

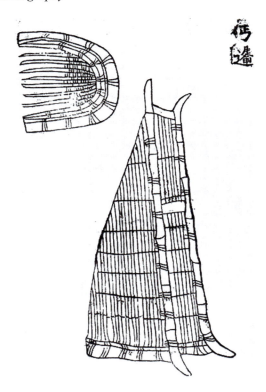

Figure 9.44 **"Cái dó"** (fishing equipment with shafts, pushed along on runners, for catching shrimps and small fish). Oger, 1909, p. 412.

and woven in the same way from thin strips of bamboo. An inverted cone shaped flap closes the opening and prevents the catch from trying to escape.

The name in Figure 9.44 is imprecise, as this fishing equipment is more like "nhủi" for catching small fishes and little shrimps. The fisherman pushes it along by holding the two handles shaped from the ends of the bamboo trunks. The device scrapes the bed of an arroyo, preferably against the current: shrimps and small fish swim into it at the open end and are caught against the latticed base without being able to escape. In the illustration, the instrument is resting on its wide base (the insert at the top of the drawing shows the shape of the base, helping to explain the way the device is used).

Equipment to catch small fish and shrimps called "đó" (Figure 9.45). It is a trap with the opening placed to receive the flow of the current and is held in place with three pointed rods rammed into the river bed. The little fish and shrimps are swept in by the current, are caught there and cannot escape.

In Figure 9.46, the "carafe-shaped trap (nơm)" is a bow-net for use in a shallow pond, stream or river. Dressed only in a loincloth, here the fisherman is holding a bow-net in both hands. He is about to plunge it into the bed of the stream. Then, he can put his right hand through the opening at the top to feel whether there is a

Basket-making 191

Figure 9.45 Fish trap with shafts. Đào Xá Village. Phú Thọ Province. 1982. Photograph by Đinh Trọng Hiếu.

Figure 9.46 "*Catching fish with a device* with the vernacular name **cái nơm** (carafe [fishing])". Oger, 1909, p. 377.

192 *Bamboo iconography*

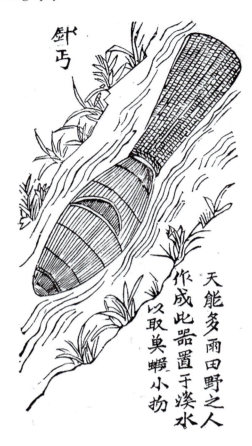

Figure 9.47 **"Cái chũm"** (traps for catching shrimps and fish). (When it is raining hard, people working in the fields make a trap like this that is placed on the stream bed to catch small shrimps and fish.) Oger, 1909, p. 115.

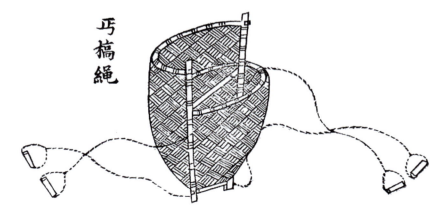

Figure 9.48 **"Cái gầu thừng"** (bailer with rope handles). Oger, 1909, p. 422.

Figure 9.49 **"Vỉ cất gầu"** ("vỉ" – pliable bamboo basket – used for irrigation). Oger, 1909, p. 384.

captive fish. If there is, he grabs it and puts it in his basket, then moves forward a few paces to repeat the procedure.

In Figure 9.47, the fish trap is set down against the current (flowing here from the top of the drawing). It is made with two clearly distinct elements: an end "carafe (nơm)" part woven from thin bamboo rods in the shape of a rocket, the open end of which is inserted in a "trap open at both ends (chũm)". The current sends good-sized fish into the "chũm", which guides the fish into the "carafe" part. There is a side opening on the rocket-shaped part so that the fisherman can take out the biggest fish, while leaving the shrimps in the water for the moment. These traps must be firmly fixed in place to avoid being carried away by the current, but this detail is not shown here.

In Figures 9.48–49, the woven bamboo container "gầu giai" is used for irrigating deep paddy fields.[18] It is made from slim bamboo slats strengthened and held in shape with a framework. The two pairs of rope handles are fixed ingeniously "head to tail", each pair for one person. It requires great skill to use this implement: time and practice are needed before a good level of efficiency is reached. The two workers use it together, swinging it like a pendulum in a continuous movement.

194 *Bamboo iconography*

Figure 9.50 **"Tát gầu sòng"** (using a bailer for irrigation). Oger, 1909, p. 612.

When the bailer hits the water in a lower paddy field, one of the workers pulls on his lower rope; the bailer sinks, fills and comes up again in a continuous movement. On the upper paddy field, the other worker pulls on his lower rope and the water in the bailer pours out. Every time, the manoeuvre is the same. To keep the movements coordinated, singing a song gives rhythm to the actions of this complicated exercise. It can only be mastered by practising for a long time. The shape of the bailer may differ in its detail.

The three Figures (9.50–52) show the basket work "tripod bailer (gầu sòng)", sometimes named "water shovel", in the shape of a half-rocket with a handle and hung from a tripod. The water is drawn from one paddy field and poured into another at more or less the same level. The dykes separating the fields prevent the water from draining out. Scenes of paddy field irrigation such as these are often

Basket-making 195

Figure 9.51 "**Tát nước**" (draining a paddy field to irrigate another). Durand, 2011, p. 35.

Figure 9.52 "**Bộ đội tát nước giúp dân**" (to help the people, soldiers are draining one paddy field to irrigate another). Durand, 2011, p. 262.

196 *Bamboo iconography*

shown on popular prints. Propaganda posters show "foot soldiers in the people's army (bộ đội)" in uniform and up to their knees in water, helping the population to irrigate their rice fields. Maurice Durand recorded illustration 3 in 1955. There is no similar poster showing soldiers using the other type of bailer.

Notes

1 Dumoutier, 1908, figure 17, pp. 66–7.
2 Or rather "quả cậy", the fruit of *Diospyros lotus* L., but several other *Diospyros* also have staining properties.
3 The Vietnamese call these fans "quạt châm kim (fans perforated with a needle)".
4 Dumoutier, 1908, pp. 64–7.
5 See *supra*, Chapter 5, p. 69
6 Not the same as "đò dọc", boat for sailing down river.
7 8 "thước" (0,425 x 8 = 3,4 m).
8 7 "thước" 5 "tấc" (2,975 + 0,2 = 3,175 m).
9 *PBTL*, [1977], pp. 142–4.
10 *Ibidem*, p. 165
11 See *supra*, Chapter 5, p. 71
12 These measures were recommended by Trần Tiễn Thành (1813–1883). Cf. Đào Duy Anh, 1944, p. 107.
13 *TL*, tb, q.V, f ° 14b [1672], 11th moon.
14 Wang Zhen, *Nongshu* 農書, in *Qinding siku quanshu* 欽定四庫全書, f ° 33b, in *Chinese Text Project* [Accessed: 7/04/2020].
15 *VĐLN*, q. IX, f ° 4b.
16 Wang Zhen, *Nongshu* 農書, in *Qinding siku quanshu* 欽定四庫全書, f ° 31b, in *Chinese Text Project*. [Accessed: 8/04/2020]. The last character [笯], which appears in the Nong-shu 農書, has been omitted by the copyist in the ms. of the VĐLN.
17 VĐLN, q. IX, f ° 4b.
18 Already in the 17th century, the *Chi nam ngọc âm giải nghĩa* dictionary (f ° 30b) differe-niated between two types of bailer, "tripod bailer (gầu sòng)" et "bailer held with ropes (gầu giai)": "薩渃莱滝宁渕薩渃莱帶 Tát nước gầu sòng. Giữa dòng tát nước gầu giai".

10 The Gia Định Art School contribution

So far in this work, more than 100 woodcuts collected by Henri Oger have been presented. They are the work of local craftsmen for whom no art school training was available in the early 20th century. Not only was their outlook limited to the rural life in the north of Vietnam in the main, but the absence of perspective in their descriptions also rendered the result somewhat awkward, in spite of great attention to detail and skilled draughtsmanship. In the south of Vietnam, from 1913 onwards, the Gia Định Art School was established; talented, young students received training in drawing, engraving and lithography. Importantly, the principal of the School, Jules-Gustave Besson, encouraged the fledgling artists to return to their villages and to record the scenes of daily life there that they considered worthy of observation and invest this potential subject matter with their conception of the beautiful. The result was a boom in the number of plates published in the form of lithographs from 1935 onwards and which cover nearly all the main aspects of daily life in Cochinchina at the time. From the extant 240 plates, a tiny number have been chosen for this chapter – 12 in all – where the subject matter is bamboo but not in any way a repetition of the themes in the Oger collection.

Bamboo has multiple uses, and although Vietnam is a country stretching out over a wide latitudinal, there are no regional objects made specifically from one sort of bamboo rather than another. Although some bamboo varieties are local, their use as a material is never specifically southern. The differences between southern and northern products are not due to a regional particularity of the material but rather to socio-cultural factors.

DOI: 10.4324/9781003350347-13

198 *Bamboo iconography*

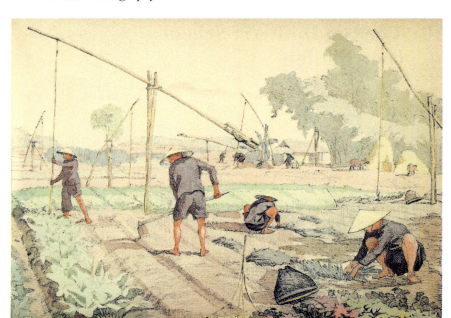

Figure 10.1 "Vegetable growing in Bình-Tây". *Monographie*, vol. 1, pl. 24 (unsigned). Bamboo rocker for drawing water from a well. Consisting of a whole bamboo trunk, fixed onto two bamboo posts and fitted with a counterweight, a bucket of water can be raised with a minimum of effort. Called "cần vọt", this system for drawing water is little used in the north, whereas it is omnipresent in the centre and in the south. Often, instead of a rope, a bamboo pole is attached to the bucket to draw the water. However, this system only works when the water table is at the same level or below the level of the rocker. It should be noted that the "cần vọt" system is similar to the Egyptian shaduf.

Figure 10.2 "Loading paddy rice into sacks". *Monographie*, vol. 4, pl. 28 (signed "Phu" below left).

From the scaffolding at the rear to the tripod supporting a basket, everything is made of bamboo. And what about the basket with the bits of straw poking through the spaces in the basketwork? It is probably some kind filter or sieve to remove bits of straw mixed up in the paddy rice before bagging up. To be compared with the Chinese "shai gu guai" (see Figure 9.33).

200 *Bamboo iconography*

Figure 10.3 "Monkey bridge" over a rạch [arroyo] at Sadec. *Monographie*, vol. 1, pl. 5 (unsigned). This is a familiar scene in the countryside in the south, where arroyos are a common feature of the landscape. Such "monkey bridges" are found all over Vietnam, but they are usually much more basic than this one, whereas this model demonstrates the prosperity of the inhabitants, shown by the solid props firmly supporting the bridge, with two hand rails at the sides. The careful placing of the bamboo props also shows a clear interest in the aesthetics of the structure.

Figure 10.4 "Large, square dipping net". *Monographie*, vol. 5, pl. 24 (signed "Phụ" below, left). A familiar fishing scene with gear that is commonly used in Việt Nam, but here, the circumstances are unusual: whereas, in general, this "large square dipping net (cái vó)" is fixed to a boat that moves, here, it is part of a hut installed in the middle of a lake. A fisherman has come to raise the dipping net. The difference is explained by the ownership status of the lake: whereas boats with a built-in dipping net fish in public waters, this illustration shows a private waterway belonging to the owner of both the hut and the dipping net.

202 *Bamboo iconography*

Figure 10.5 "Threshing rice". *Monographie*, vol. 4, pl. 23 (signed "Kiem", lower right). The upper part of the equipment used to remove the grain from the stalks of rice is made of woven bamboo. Its generous size and shape are intended to prevent the grain from scattering. It is being used in the context of semi-mechanized production in the prosperous rice-growing areas of the south. As shown here, the machine is not used singly but is part of a battery. Other hands are busy tying up the threshed rice stalks into sheaves.

The Gia Định Art School contribution 203

Figure 10.6 "Hulling rice". *Monographie*, vol. 4, pl. 30 (signed "Kiem", lower right). This is the same "hulling mill (cối xay lúa)" as everywhere else in the country, but it is larger in size and worked by two women farmers. To be compared with Figure 9.37.

204   *Bamboo iconography*

Figure 10.7 "Making bamboo grinders for separating rice from its straw". *Monographie*, vol. 4, pl. 17 (signed "Quan" lower right).

It is rare to find an illustration of these grinders for hulling. (There is a mistake in the title, however: this grinder is used to remove the husks from the grains. At this stage of the conditioning process, any "straw" has already been removed.) In the north, artisans would make one or two of these grinders to order, whereas here, it appears that they are perhaps producing them in large numbers. The blades inserted in the surfaces of the grinder are made of the best quality cortical layer of bamboo, which is extremely hard. Even so, they wear out very quickly, not only due to the friction as the grinder turns but also because they split open the grains of paddy rice to remove the husk, which contains silica. Compare with Figure 9.39.

The Gia Định Art School contribution 205

Figure 10.8 "Winnowing rice". *Monographie*, vol. 4, pl. 28b (signed "Trung" lower left). Unlike the rest of the country, southern Việt Nam produces a large surplus quantity of rice, as illustrated in this drawing. Winnowing is the next process after hulling: the hulled rice still includes the husks of the paddy rice. As they are lighter, these outer husks are removed by winnowing. This "winnow (máy quạt thóc)" is being operated by a woman who is covered from head to toe to protect her from the resultant dust. The paddy rice would have been stocked in enormous "basket ware silos (lẫm)" in the background, far larger than the silos in the north ("cót thóc", or "cót vựa"). Porters are bringing baskets of this rice mixed with husks to feed into the winnowing machine. This equipment for stocking known as "lẫm", often paired with "đụn"[1], is used to indicate either the container for rice or the place where it is kept.[2]

206   *Bamboo iconography*

Figure 10.9 "Poultry seller". *Monographie*, vol. 1, pl. 29 (signed "Đạt", lower left).
This hens' cage is surprisingly large. The lithograph renderings by the students of the Gia Định Art School have several advantages when compared to the monochrome wood engravings. Thirty years separates Oger's (1909) woodblock prints from the Gia Định students, who, having been trained in the laws of perspective, allowed themselves daring and sometimes subtle composition, as shown here in the detail of the basketwork and the outlines of the poultry seen through the open weave of the basket.

The Gia Định Art School contribution 207

Figure 10.10 "A Nhà-quê (peasant) comes home from market carrying her nho [nhỏ] (child) in her basket". *Monographie*, vol. 6, pl. 3 (unsigned).
Both the carrying pole and the two deep baskets ("thúng") are made of bamboo. The straps, made from rattan cane, are more supple and last longer than the bamboo equivalent. This form of transport using a small child as a counterweight to the goods is not exclusive to the south.

208   *Bamboo iconography*

Figure 10.11 "A corner in the kitchen with utensils". *Monographie*, vol. 2, pl. 27 (signed "P. Tri", lower left).

The laconic title does not give a fair idea of how unusual the scene is: as well as the roof structure, made entirely of bamboo, the drawing shows a large kitchen where two old-style fireplaces are installed on an insulated stand so that the cook can work standing up instead of crouching down to operate at floor level. The bamboo basket-ware hanging above the hearth will benefit from a daily smoking, protecting it from being attacked by insects. Several holders have been created in a thick bamboo trunk so that kitchen utensils (chopsticks, spatulas, ladles) are always to hand for the cook. This sort of "cutlery container" is found from the north of the Central region (Nghệ-Tĩnh) right down to the far south of the country.

Figure 10.12 "Cupping", (market scene). *Monographie*, vol. 2, pl. 18 (signed "Luu-cong" lower right).

This drawing by a student of the Art School at Gia Định (1935) was made 20 years before the photograph taken by Raymond Cauchetier.[3] A "surgery" is taking place at the market; a patient with his back bared is seated on a low stool, just like the healer, a bearded man of a venerable age. A teapot is placed on an earthenware charcoal burner (a standard portable version updated in the south) and the old man is using chopsticks to remove short lengths of bamboo (closed at one end by the diaphragm) from the hot water. He empties the water out of the tube and places it on the patient's back. The cooling of the air in the tube creates suction on the skin. A reddish or purplish mark appears on the skin. It should be remembered that one of the principles of traditional medicine is to visualize the problem, trying to bring an interior problem to the surface by making it visible on the outside of the body thereby controlling it and so healing it. Instead of using glass suction cups that are difficult to make or more costly, bamboo tubes are used. The elderly lady on the photograph taken by Raymond Cauchetier is doing exactly the same thing. The little boy whose back is covered with tubes does not appear to be suffering much. What is exactly the illness that the cupping treatment is supposed to cure? As a remedy, these locally produced suction cups ("đặt ống giác") are supposed to relieve underlying pain problems from rheumatism to discomfort from indigestion. Their use does not present any danger, except that caution is necessary to avoid a burn or any wound infection resulting from over-frequent use of such cupping. At present, various websites explain that this treatment has developed from the use of moxa in traditional scholarly Chinese medicine. This is by no means certain.

210 *Bamboo iconography*

A case of socialization of bamboo, where the naming "bamboo" indicates a social category

Vương Hồng Sển, again in his dictionary, at the definition for "Ba nhe" and "Bán bù" – two social categories in southern Việt Nam during French colonial rule. "Ba nhe" comes from the word "panier" ("basket" in French), meaning a bamboo basket used by children at the market place. As soon as they saw a French woman coming to do her shopping, they offered to carry her purchases back to her carriage and/or her house, in exchange for a tip. For the Vietnamese, the using of this nickname had a derogatory connotation for the children doing this sort of job.[4]

The author is even clearer in his attitude towards the "Bán Bù", a name derived from the French "bambou" and used for adults (whereas "Ba nhe" applies only to children). The "Bán Bù" were mainly scoundrels, members of a fraternity of carriers who did not hesitate to wield their carrying poles to acquire a clientele. They used large bamboo baskets (called "cần xé") for this work and, as their loads were heavier, the payment they received was higher. While a teacher earned 5–6 piasters a month, the "Bán bù" could line their pockets with up to 0,50 piaster a day, even though they were looked down on by the inhabitants.[5]

Notes

1 Lê Quý Đôn is alluding to "đụn". *VĐLN*, q. X, f ° 4a.
2 Huình Tịnh Paulus Của, vol. 1, 1895, p. 331.
3 Cauchetier, Raymond, *Saigon*, Paris: Albin Michel, 1955, p. 64. See also https://raymond-cauchetier.com/blog/galerie/vietnam/ [Accessed: 5/04/2023].
4 Vương Hồng Sển, 1993, pp. 49–50.
5 *Ibidem*, pp. 58–9.

Part 3

Contemporary bamboo

11 Bamboo at present

Two photographs that follow give an idea of the possible outcomes for the future of bamboo and its by-products in Vietnam. These two pictures were taken 12 years apart. The first, by the mathematician Klaus Krickeberg, was taken in Hà Nội around 1978. It shows a shopkeeper surrounded by her display of everyday household utensils. Apart from two grey plastic baskets, all the rest is made of plant material, mostly bamboo (with the exception of the feather duster). No shop display nowadays could offer such a range of articles – and in such number. The damaging impact on the environment of plastic, which is not readily biodegradable, ought to allow a free rein to the return of plant materials such as bamboo.

However, it is fairly improbable that this will happen. Indeed, over the last 60 years, not only plastic but also cement, concrete and aluminium have replaced bamboo. War and chemical spraying (particularly defoliants) have had a serious effect on the allocation of land surface devoted to bamboo, irrespective of whether it grows naturally or has been cultivated. The countryside and suburban areas and, indeed, any populated spot where bamboo was predominant are all much changed.

Taken recently, the second photograph is just as interesting: the use of bamboo has not been abandoned, but the crafts that use it as a material have become specialized. The plant is no longer omnipresent as before; the traditional hedging in the north and in the south is now only a rare survivor. Distant villages where bamboo is plentiful take charge of planting, felling, cutting and then sending it to basket-making villages nearer to large urban centres. Only two or three of the most popular sorts of "fish trap (đó)" are made there. Traditional bamboo crafts are still practised, but they are no longer seen as having a promising future.

However, at present, consumers' preoccupations tend to be directed more towards the aesthetics of bamboo; for example, Figure 11.3 on the following page showing a screen in a home of the Kà-tu ethnic minority, which allows a beautiful quality light into the living space while protecting the privacy of the inhabitants.

Indeed, some entrepreneurs have been exploring the various possibilities for using bamboo as textile fibre or for making paper. Without wishing to pass

DOI: 10.4324/9781003350347-15

214　*Contemporary bamboo*

Figure 11.1 Display of household goods in front of a "hardware" shop. Hà Nội, *circa* 1978. Photograph by Klaus Krickeberg.

Figure 11.2 "Bamboo fish traps (đó) seller waiting for the ferry to Uông Bí jetty, Bạch Đằng River", 1990. Photograph by Nicolas Cornet.

Figure 11.3 Woven bamboo screens in a Kà-tu home. Kà-tu Eco-museum, Huế. 2003. Photograph by Đinh Trọng Hiếu.

judgement on the future of such attempts, which have already shown somewhat inconclusive results, in favour of bamboo, it can be clearly demonstrated as a renewable and readily available material. Although less profitable than planting rubber trees, a bamboo plantation requires much less investment in terms of labour costs and maintenance. As a "savings bank" for the villager who has it growing in his garden, as a "tool box" for the handyman who has some at home or easily obtainable, bamboo may well become the favoured material for sustainable crafts: for furniture making such as that in Xuân Lai village[1] using burnt bamboo, for toys or bicycles that can all be made from this natural material, one that is cheap, pliable, durable and biodegradable. Some astute and enthusiastic craftsmen there are already finding such work very profitable.[2]

Bamboo is also used in other unexpected ways; for example, as equipment for action by the special brigade of the Vietnamese police force when they need to occupy a building; the men can climb walls as if they have some kind of magic adhesive sole on their boots. In fact, each commando leans on a stout bamboo pole held by two aides, the pole holds him against the wall and he can then climb up the wall as if he were walking along a (vertical) street. This is thanks to two almost contradictory qualities of bamboo: strength and pliability. Of course, it would be possible to manufacture a similar device relying on synthetic materials, but it is quicker and much cheaper to just fell one or two of the bamboo trunks that grow so profusely in the damp, tropical climate.

Architects are exploiting to a maximum the qualities of bamboo, not only for installing scaffolding that does not initially inspire confidence but also for contemporary buildings made of plant material, combining the advantages of low cost, availability, pliability, shock-absorbent and even anti-seismic structures. Honours should be awarded to the Vietnamese architect Võ Trọng Nghĩa for having found the way to transform an existing shop space into an attractive pavilion to accommodate cultural exchange events at Expo 2010 Shanghai, China. Since then, the architectural creations of Võ Trọng Nghĩa have become known the world over, not only for modernity of form but also for the folksy character and warmth that emanate from their decoration. The architect has admitted his preference for a species of bamboo that he considers typical among all those that grow in Vietnam – the *Bambusa variabilis* Munro ("tầm vông"). The tree, growing to medium height (10–15m), has an almost solid trunk and so is very strong, but at the same time, it is regular in shape and is more pliable than any other variety. It grows on unpromising terrain and has the particularity of becoming even harder the more the conditions are unfavourable. Such qualities made it a simple but fearsome weapon in times gone by when it was also used to make sharpened stakes to defend villages from attack. At present, the architect has inherited, so to speak, a material that has not only stood the test of time but is also deeply anchored in popular symbolism, and he uses it to design buildings that are in keeping with modernity.

Figure 11.4 "Vietnam" Pavilion at Expo 2010 Shanghai, China. Photograph by Võ Trọng Nghĩa.

Bamboo at present 217

Figure 11.5 "Wind and Water (Gió và Nước)" Bar at Bình Dương, 2013. Photograph by Võ Trọng Nghĩa.

Figure 11.6 Interior decoration of the "Wind and Water" Bar, 2006. Photograph by Võ Trọng Nghĩa.[3]

218 *Contemporary bamboo*

Figure 11.7 Kaly Tran and lithophone with bamboo sound box. 2018. *Screen shot*. Available: www.youtube.com/watch?v=dz02zLU9oU8 [Accessed: 15/06/2019].

One of these young musicians from the Bahnar ethnic minority, Kaly Tran, is a virtuoso on the lithophone and on other traditional instruments, such as the "đàn t'rưng". He enjoys performing his interpretations by not taking himself too seriously and gives the audience the opportunity to listen to a fresh rendering of old tunes. Enjoy the style of Kaly Tran, a young musician who brings out sounds like no other from bamboo. Here, it is to celebrate the investiture of a new bishop in Kontum.

In a completely different context, for those who manage to read the signs, bamboo may well be a plant that inspires hope. The ethnic minority populations of the Highlands of Vietnam are known for using bamboo to make musical instruments.[4] This has been shown in the work of several ethnologists, including Georges Condominas and Jacques Dournes, who collected, described and published work on many different bamboo percussion instruments, not to mention other types of musical instruments. Now, after their field work in the 1960's among these groups, a new survey should be carried out, to include the numerous instruments that have since been created in these areas.

Not only the instruments themselves but also the musical ensembles or the occasions when this music is played: solo, duet, group, during street processions or for the investiture of a new prelate, with such enthusiasm, vigour and with such

Figure 11.8 Kaly Tran, performing one of his compositions on the "đàn t'rưng (bamboo xylophone)" for "celebrating the investiture of a new bishop in Kon Tum". 2016. *Screen shot.* Available: www.youtube.com/watch?v=OEA6NBb3U38 [Accessed: 15/06/2019].

fervour and skill that all hopes are allowed for a social group displaying such admirable creativity.

Notes

1 It is part of the commune with the same name (sub-prefecture of Gia Bình, Bắc Ninh Province). Fanchette, 2009, pp. 166–71.
2 Available: htps://congthuong.vn/bien-tre-gai-thanh-khung-xe-dap-xuat-khau-19588.html [Accessed: 15/06/2019].
3 Available: https://kienviet.net/2012/06/27/gian-hang-viet-nam-tai-trien-lam-expro-thuong-hai-nam-2010-cong-ty-tnhh-vo-trong-nghia/ [Accessed: 15/06/2019].
4 See *supra*, Chapter 3, pp. 49–54.

Conclusion

What status for bamboo?

Technological development in the 21st century has had inevitable repercussions on the use of bamboo. However, nowhere in Việt Nam has it been completely abandoned to the benefit of plastics, whose polyvalence is equivalent or even superior to this plant. The reason for this is simple: it is available most of the time, reproducing itself in the wild or in gardens, so it can be acquired for very little cost. Clearly, there is even positive development in two areas where creativity goes hand in hand with enhancing the intrinsic qualities of the bamboo. As we have seen earlier, these domains are music and architecture, using, respectively, the sound quality and the possibilities offered for creating shape and volume.

Even so, most of the time, craftwork production using bamboo is limited to utilitarian objects and pays little attention to the beauty of the material, which is a shame. Artisans produce objects intended for everyday use for a market where aesthetic considerations are less important than low prices. Usually, the finish of a brand-new bamboo article is rarely satisfactory; it is constant use that imparts not only a patina but also a certain beautiful je-ne-sais-quoi. Although the everyday utensil may not be particularly beautiful to start with, it can, indeed, become so. Here, the aesthetic dimension, which generally provides the artisan with a certain status, is totally lacking during the transaction. It is only present when the object is created for personal use. There is a socio-historic reason at the root of this attitude. It was clearly analysed by Doctor Hocquard at the time of the Tonkin conquest. He is quoted below to provide a better understanding of Vietnamese craftwork in general, even though he is not referring specifically to crafts using bamboo.

> He (the artisan) is merely copying, in a more or less slavish way, a given model, and, but for the rare exception, he doesn't copy it particularly well. He takes no initiative and is not an artist in the same way as the Chinese worker or more importantly the Japanese worker. I do not mean to say that he is not capable of doing work as well as they: I believe that he cannot be bothered because he will only lose out by being too good a worker. Indeed in Japan, the artist who, after years of toil, produces a work of beauty is well regarded by all his compatriots, who respect him as a master of his art. In Tonkin on the other hand, when an artisan has produced a remarkable work in his field of competence, the local chief immediately reports to the mandarin of the

DOI: 10.4324/9781003350347-16

Conclusion 221

province who then immediately informs the king. Then, one day, on an order from Hué, this skilled workman is suddenly separated from his family and sent to the capital. He is held captive in one of the royal palaces: he is kept busy there for the rest of his life working at the court in return for a paltry retribution, often enhanced by a stroke of the cane. With such customs, it is understandable that artists in Tonkin hide their talent with as much care as the workmen in other countries take to display theirs.[1]

Bamboo is intrinsically a grass and therefore cannot escape its condition. Sometimes considered to be a tree due to its significant height (sometimes 30 or 40m) – a dimension not always attained by woody plants – it remains a grass. As such, and with no outside intervention, it renews itself yearly and remains evergreen. Grasses do not age; they grow, spread, survive adverse weather conditions, then die and renew after several years, often unremarked. Bamboo does not register a memory in its fibres, as is the case for true ligneous plants; it disappears without ever achieving the venerability usually conferred by age and years. Although the Vietnamese designate it using the term "tree ('cây tre')", it is not truly a tree, either by its structure or its condition. It dies after several years and is replaced by its numerous young shoots.

This is the fundamental difference with a real tree.

Note

1 Hocquard, 1892, p. 36. It should be noted that the first imperial manufactures (bách tác 百作) date from the Lý dynasty (1009–1225). The dynastic histories refer to them in 1146 (*TT*, bản kỷ, q. IV, f ° 5b). They were restored in the 15th century under the Later Lê. Under the rule of inspectors, artisans were subject to severe regulation as stipulated by several articles in the Lê Code.

Annexes

I. Input from texts and the field. The case of vegetable salts: from ginger to bamboo

Often, in our research into early texts, we encountered problems that could not be resolved by simply using the exegesis of other documents. At this point, the contribution of fieldwork is crucial to understanding an issue, one that may, in fact, be demonstrated as quite simple. One clear example illustrates this and remains within the framework of our research into the uses of bamboo.

A terse phrase in *Selection of Strange Tales in Lĩnh Nam* (15th cent.) on the customs of the early Vietnamese, five Chinese characters 以薑根爲鹽 transcribed into Sino-Vietnamese "dĩ khương căn vi diêm", and there being no variant in any other document available to us[1], the meaning is accepted unanimously in Vietnam: making salt from ginger root. Word for word: take/ginger/root/make/salt. However, there had never been an attempt at explanation, until a historian[2] ventured to translate the five words into French: "[The population made] preserves of ginger root". This mistranslation is explained by a lack of knowledge of how to produce vegetable salts. Without this translation and mistranslation, our understanding of the matter would have remained unclear.

The technique for obtaining vegetable salts is well known. It consists in incinerating plants in order to produce potassic substitutes for dietary sodium chloride from the ashes. Roland Portères, ethno-botanist at Muséum National d'Histoire Naturelle, mentions that, in the forests of French Guinea, Zingiberaceae (*Costus lucasianus* J. Brown et K. Schum., and *Costus afer* Ker.) were used for producing cooking salt by this method.[3] He also notes that the ethnologist Georges Condominas provided information on a similar usage in Indochina. The Khmer-speaking Rlam tribe (Mnong group), to the north of Dalat, gather an aquatic water plant ("kùl") with narrow leaves. It is dried in a similar manner to tobacco. The ash is lixivated. The filtrate is boiled and reduced; the paste obtained is left to dry. The resultant salt is exchanged at the rate of a good handful for a 12kg of paddy rice.[4] These details help to solve the "mystery" of the early text and demonstrate that, at the time, the Việt population had not yet reached the lower coastal areas where the method for obtaining sea salt is different.[5] So far, there is no obvious connection with the study of bamboo. But during fieldwork, on a third visit to Đào Xá Village, from June to November 1989, tiring of asking the same question of scholars in and outside the country and never having received any satisfactory answer, I (Đ.T.H.) repeated the question to the elderly peasant who had already been our host in 1982. Rather than being surprised, he replied calmly:

> People in the Highlands of our country did not have sea salt like they do nowadays. They took bamboo with a thin outside layer ("nứa") for burning. When the fire reached as far as the diaphragm, the bamboo was put out and the ashes were put aside, then another section was burned in the same way, and so on. The mixture was heated until it was completely dried out. The result was a substance similar to salt" (25/09/1989).[6]

In his youth, this peasant had travelled and so had met with ethnic minority groups near Đào Xá Village, situated in the Midlands in the north of Vietnam. His curiosity and his keen observation helped us to understand several issues, which without his contribution would have remained problematic. He often made drawings on the paving in the rice-drying courtyard, so that the researcher could easily copy them into his notebook. Often, when fieldwork notes are supported by a drawing, it is easiier to understand the complexity of the mechanism of an agricultural machine (with the naming of each of its parts) or to see how fire is made by rubbing a sliver of bamboo against wood.

The interaction between texts and terrain are not restricted to our examples or to these sketches, as shown by Emmanuel Poisson concerning the Vietnamese encyclopaedist Lê Quý Đôn.[7] In the future, it would be interesting to establish whether the latter and the botanist Joannis de Loureiro were ever in contact, both of them having carried out fieldwork in the same area at the same period. Indeed, it would be surprising if they hadn't met.

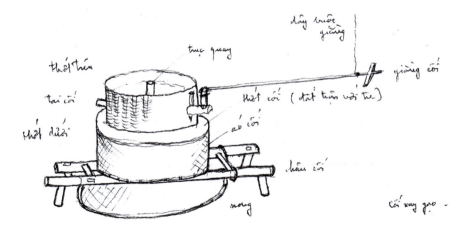

Figure 12.1 Grinder, its parts and their names. Drawing by Đinh Trọng Hiếu.

224 *Annexes*

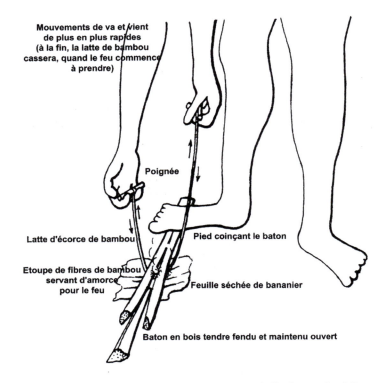

Figure 12.2 Making fire by rubbing a sliver of bamboo on wood. Drawing by Đinh Trọng Hiếu.

II. Making, buying

The inventory of the uses of bamboo in Vietnam presented in the book is as complete as possible, seen from the "technological" point of view: bamboo in its natural state, bamboo after transformation. But this limits the uses to one aspect while ignoring the inter-relational element; for example, which items are bought; which are manufactured. The answers open further perspectives. The photograph of the "sacrificial knife", taken at the Nguyễn Văn Huyên Ethnographic Museum, the bell for buffalo or the hen coop are all made locally in small numbers.

In the same way, an enclosure for rearing ducks will probably be homemade rather than bought. Some constructions, such as building a noria or an extensive water channel, require much technical skill, in which case the wider community of neighbours and family is called upon to help.

The photograph of a cyclist transporting dozens of fish traps[8] introduces a further consideration: craftwork, previously and sometimes still produced within the

Figure 12.3 Sacrificial knife for buffalo. Vietnam Museum of Ethnology. 2003. Photograph by Đinh Trọng Hiếu.

Figure 12.4 Bell for buffalo. Vietnam Museum of Ethnology. 2003. Photograph by Đinh Trọng Hiếu.

home, is tending to become more commonly available in the marketplace. For over a century, markets have been held where such products were sold as they still are in contemporary Vietnam, with artisans working together in village "Cooperatives".

In these scenes that can be dated simply by observing the changes in dress (and/or headdress) between the 1920s and nowadays, the same variety of baskets, flakes and racks of all sizes whose main common characteristic is the pale colour of the products before they acquire the patina of use and wear, giving the product the clear status of a bought product but that the new owner, having paid for it at the market stall, has already honoured by removing the sharp barbs of the bamboo, providing an aesthetic element lacking in the raw product. From enlargements of several photographs taken at various markets at different times, one can observe, unfortunately, the "ugliness" of certain new bamboo products sold in markets that have been roughly cut by knife, leaving uneven surfaces that are dangerous to use

226 *Annexes*

Figure 12.5 Hen coop. Đào Xá Village. Phú Thọ Province, 1982. Photograph by Đinh Trọng Hiếu.

Figure 12.6 Scene at a basket-ware market. Northern Vietnam. Details. Circa 1920. ANOM. Service Photographique du Gouvernement Général de l'Indochine.

Annexes 227

Figure 12.7 New, roughly cut carrying poles. Photograph by Đinh Trọng Hiếu.

Figure 12.8 New, carafe-shaped traps, sold at market. Vinh market, 1979. Details. Photograph by Đinh Trọng Hiếu.

Figure 12.9 Carafe-shaped trap made by Nguyễn Văn Thái, Đào Xá Village. Phú Thọ Province. 1982. Photograph by Đinh Trọng Hiếu.

Figure 12.10 Hook made in one piece from base of bamboo trunk made by Venerable Hà Liên. Đào Xá Village. Phú Thọ Province. 1982. Photograph by Đinh Trọng Hiếu.

because of their sharp edges. This, indeed, shows the difference between the careful bamboo craftwork techniques passed from father to son, as in Japan, for example, and the production of cheap everyday objects swiftly made and quickly sold in Vietnam, in the past and in the present day.

Nevertheless, a tradition, although it is sadly weakened now, still carries on: the beautiful object created for personal use or as a collector's item. Earlier, the photographs show fish traps on sale at market: very different but made with the same basket-weaving technique the fish trap shown here was made for personal use and has been discreetly decorated with rattan wands. Another example is the hook made from old bamboo, polished with age and wear and displayed proudly as a "beauty". Jacques Dournes, who hardly mentions the "wood-bamboo" distinction, brought back from his sojourn with the Jarai people beautiful and interesting examples of craftwork in bamboo and in "bamboo root" (or "mature base of bamboo" where the roots form) as well as worn stone adzes. These are all listed in old Catalogues du Musée de l'Homme.

Notes

1 Apart from ms. 0652. Cf. Vũ Quỳnh, Kiều Phú, *Lĩnh Nam chích quái liệt truyên* 嶺南摭怪列傳, q. I, f ° 6a, in *The Vietnamese Nôm Preservation Foundation* [Accessed: 2/02/2020].
2 This was Lê Thành Khôi. Đinh, 1985–1986, pp. 6–25.
3 Portère, 1950, p. 54.
4 *Ibidem*, p. 35.
5 On the production of sea salt in Thuận Hóa, cf. *PBTL*, [1977], pp. 140–1.
6 Đinh, 1992, pp. 5–37.
7 Poisson, 2017, pp. 59–70.
8 See, *supra*, p. 212, Figure 11.2.

Bibliography

Sites

Bibliothèque nationale de France, *Gallica*. Available: https://gallica.bnf.fr.
British Library. Available: www.bl.uk/manuscripts/.
Chinese Text Project (Baijia zhuzi 百家諸子). Available: https://ctext.org/.
Chữ Nôm Resources. Available: www.chunom.org.
Library of Congress. Available: www.loc.gov.
Notes du Mont royal. Available: www.notesdumontroyal.com
The Vietnamese Nôm Preservation Foundation. Available: www.nomfoundation.org.
Viện nghiên cứu Hán Nôm. Available: www.hannom.org.vn.
Việt Nam từ điển. Available: http://hanviet.org.free.fr

Dictionaries

***Chỉ nam ngọc âm giải nghĩa* 指南玉音解義 [Explanation of the Guide to Jeweled Sounds], 17th cent., Hà Nội: Viện nghiên cứu Hán Nôm, AB. 372.
*Đỗ Tất Lợi, *Những cây thuốc và vị thuốc Việt Nam* [Medicinal Plants and Substances in Việt Nam], Hà Nội: Nhà xuất bản Khoa học và Kỹ thuật, 4th revised and completed edition, 1981.
*Génibrel, Jean-François-Marie, *Dictionnaire annamite-français*, Saigon: Impr. de la Mission à Tân Định, 1898. See also in *Chữ Nôm Resources*. Available: https://chunom.org/pages/genibrel/#1
*Huình Tịnh Paulus Của, 大南國音字彙 *Đại Nam Quấc Âm Tự Vị – Dictionnaire annamite*, Saigon: Rey et Curiol, vol. 1, 1895. See also in *Việt Nam từ điển*. Available: http://hanviet.org.free.fr/dnqatv/index.html
*Lê Khả Kế et al., *Cây cỏ thường thấy ở Việt Nam* [Plants often found in Việt Nam]. 6 vol., vol. 5, Bambusoïdeae, Hà Nội: Nhà xuất bản Khoa học và Kỹ thuật, 1975.
*Nguyễn Hữu Vinh et al., *Tự điển chữ Nôm trích dẫn – Dictionary of Nôm characters with excerps*, Westminster, CA: Viện Việt học, 2009. See also in *Việt Nam từ điển*. Available: http://hanviet.org.free.fr/chunom-trichdan/index.html
*Nguyễn Lân, *Tự điển thành ngữ và tục ngữ Việt Nam* [Dictionary of Vietnamese Sayings and Proverbs], Hà Nội: Nhà xuất bản văn hóa, 1989.
*Nguyễn Quang Hồng, *Khái luận văn tự học chữ Nôm* [Vietnamese vernacular writing – a philological overview], Thành phố Hồ Chí Minh: Nhà xuất bản Giáo dục, 2008.
*Nguyễn Quang Hồng, *Tự điển chữ Nôm dẫn giải*, Hà Nội: Nhà xuất bản Khoa học xã hội, 2 vol., 2015. See also in *The Vietnamese Nôm Preservation Foundation*. Available: http://www.nomfoundation.org./nom-tools/Tu-Dien-Chu-Nom-Dan_Giai?uiLang=en

*Phạm Hoàng Hộ, *Cây cỏ Việt Nam* [*An Illustrated Flora of Vietnam*], Santa Ana, CA, 1991–1993, 3 vol., vol. 3, part 2: *Poaceae- Bambuseae.*

*Rhodes, Alexandre de, *Dictionarivm Annnamiticvm Lvsitanvm, et Latinvm ope Sacræ Congregationis de Propaganda Fide in lvcem editvm ab Alexandro de Rhodes e' Societate Iesv, eiusdem Sacræ Congregationis Missionario Apostolico*, Rome: Stamperia della Sacra Congregazione de Propaganda Fide, 1651, 900 p. + Appendix + Index Latini Sermonis AB-VX. Translated into Vietnamese by Thanh Lãng, Hoàng Xuân Việt, Đỗ Quang Chính. Thành phố Hồ Chí Minh: Nhà xuất bản Khoa học Xã hội, 1991.

*Trần Trọng Dương, *Nguyễn Trãi Quốc âm từ điển* 阮廌國音辭典 [A Dictionary of *Poems in the speech of the Kingdom* by Nguyễn Trãi], Hà Nội: nhà xuất bản bách khoa, 2014.

*Vương Hồng Sển, *Tự vị tiếng Việt miền Nam* [Dictionary of the Southern Vietnamese Language], Thành phố Hồ Chí Minh: Văn hóa, 1993.

Primary sources

*Dai Kaizhi, *Zhupu* 竹譜 [Treatise on Bamboo], Waseda edition, ms. 14–00807. Available: www.wul.waseda.ac.jp [Accessed: 5/06/2020].

Đại Nam thực lục 大南寔錄 [Veritable Records of the Great South], 1844–1909, written by the State Historiography Institute, publication of the first six chronicles, Tokyo: Keio Institute of linguistic studies, 1961–1980.

Đại Việt sử ký toàn thư 大越史記全書 [Complete Book of the Historical Records of Đại Việt], reedition of the text printed in the 18th year of the Chính Hòa era (1697) followed by five additional chapters until the end of the Lê period (1789), Tokyo: Documentation Center for Asian Studies, Institute of Oriental Studies, 1984–1986.

Đồng Khánh địa dư chí 同慶地輿志 [The Descriptive Geography of the Emperor Đồng Khánh], 1887–1889, edited by Ngô Đức Thọ et al., Hà Nội: Viện nghiên cứu Hán Nôm-EFEO, 2003, 3 vol.

Hoàng Việt luật lệ 皇越律例 [Law and Regulation of Imperial Việt], 1813, in *The Vietnamese Nôm Preservation Foundation* Available: https://lib.nomfoundation.org/collection/1/search?csrfmiddlewaretoken=u9LVECX8mA9Z1C5QpP6tiI8C8POwskRIaNLFqMetJc46zLWKnGj8CAsJ6swzDSqE&query=皇越律例 [Accessed: 2/02/2020].

*Jɪ Han, *Nan-fang ts'ao mu chuang. A Fourth Century Flora of Southeast Asia*. Introduction, translation and commentaries by Li Hui-Lin, Hong Kong: The Chinese University Press, 1979.

Khâm định Việt sử thông giám cương mục 欽定越史通鑑綱目 [Imperially Commissioned Itemized Summaries of the Comprehensive Mirror of Việt History], 1884, *chính biên*, ms. 0174-19 in *The Vietnamese Preservation Nôm Foundation*. Available: https://lib.nomfoundation.org/collection/1/volume/269/ [Accessed: 15/04/2021].

*Lê Hữu Trác, *Nữ công thắng lãm* 女工勝覽 [Comprehensive Overview of Women's Work], preface 1760, transcription of the original ms. from vernacular writing into quốc ngữ by Lê Trần Đức, Viện Nghiên cứu Đông Y. Hà Nội: Phụ nữ, 1971.

*Lê Quý Đôn, *Vân Đài loại ngữ* 蕓臺類語 [Categorized Sayings from the library], 1773, Hà Nội: Viện nghiên cứu Hán Nôm, ms. A. 141.

*Lê Quý Đôn, *Lê Quý Đôn toàn tập*, t.I, *Phủ biên tạp lục* 撫邊雜錄 [Miscellaneous Chronicles of the Pacified Frontier], 1776, Hà Nội: Khoa học Xã hội, 1977.

*Lê Trắc, *An Nam chí lược* 安南志略 [Abbreviated Records of An Nam], 14th cent., Hà Nội: Viện nghiên cứu Hán Nôm, ms. A. 16.

232 *Bibliography*

*Liang Shaoren, *Liang ban qiu yu an sui bi* 兩般秋雨盦隨筆 [Random Jottings from Autumnal Rain Studio in Two Categories], in *Chinese Text Project*. Available: https://ctext.org/wiki.pl?if=gb&chapter=439310 [Accessed: 15/03/2020].

*Loureiro, Juan de, *Flora cochinchinensis*, Lisbonne: Ulyssipone: typis, et expensis academicis, 1790, 2 vol.

Lý hạng ca dao 里巷歌謠, Hà Nội: Viện nghiên cứu Hán Nôm, ms. VNv.303.

Nam quốc phương ngôn tục ngữ bị lục 南國方言俗語備錄 [Exhaustive Inventory of Sayings and Proverbs from the Southern Country], Hà Nội: Quán Văn Đường, 1914, Viện nghiên cứu Hán Nôm, ms. AB. 619, f ° 1a-48b.

*Nguyễn Binh-Khiêm, *Bạch vân am quốc ngữ thi tập* 白雲庵國語詩集, translation into French by Paul, Schneider, *Nguyễn Binh-Khiêm, porte parole de la sagesse populaire: le* Bạch vân am quốc ngữ thi tập – Recueil des poèmes en langue nationale de la Retraite du nuage blanc, Saigon: Société des études indochinoises, 1974.

*Nguyễn Du, *Truyện Kiều* 傳翹 [Tale of *Kiều*], ms. (1870) in vernacular writting in *The Vietnamese Nôm Preservation Foundation* (Available: http://www.nomfoundation.org/nom-project/tale-of-kieu/tale-of-kieu-version-1870 [Accessed: 16/08/2021]); translation into French by Nguyễn Văn Vĩnh, *Kim-Vân-Kiều*, Hanoi: Éditions Alexandre de Rhodes, 1942. See also *Notes du Mont royal*. Available: https://www.notesdumontroyal.com/document/4e.pdf [Accessed: 20/08/2021].

*Nguyễn Trãi, *Quốc âm thi tập* 國音詩集 [Collection of Poems in the Kingdom's Speech], in *Nguyễn Trãi toàn tập*, Hà Nội: Nhà xuất bản Khoa học Xã hội, 1976, pp. 395–476.

*Nguyễn Trãi, *Nguyên Trai et son recueil de poèmes en langue nationale*, étude et trad. par Paul Schneider et al., Paris: Éd. du CNRS, 1987.

*Phạm Thận Duật, *Hưng Hóa ký lược* 興化紀略 [Brief Description of Hưng Hóa], 1856, in *Phạm Thận Duật toàn tập*, Hà Nội: nhà xuất bản văn hoá thông tin, 2000.

*Su Jing, *Xinxiu bencao* 新修本草 [Newly Revised Pharmacopoeia], fac-simile of ms. dated circa 731, ed. Shanghai guji chubanshe, Shanghaï 1985.

*Tao Gu, *Qingyilu* 清異錄 [Records of Pure Marvels] in *Chinese Text Project*. Available: https://ctext.org/library.pl?if=gb&res=157 [Accessed: 16/05/2020].

*Vũ Quỳnh, Kiều Phú, *Lĩnh Nam chích quái liệt truyên* 嶺南摭怪列傳 [Selection of Strange Tales in Lĩnh Nam], ms. 0652, q.I, in *The Vietnamese Nôm Preservation Foundation*. Available: https://lib.nomfoundation.org/collection/1/volume/820/ [Accessed: 2/02/2020].

*Vũ Quỳnh, Kiều Phú, *Lĩnh Nam Chích Quái*, 15th cent., trad., Hà Nội: Nhà xuất bản Văn hóa, 1960.

*Wang Zhen, *Nongshu* 農書 [Book of Agriculture] in *Chinese Text Project*. Available: https://ctext.org/wiki.pl?if=gb&res=922992 [Accessed: 7/04/2020].

*Yuan Ke (ed.), *Shanhaijing jiaoyi* 山海經校譯 [The Classic of the Mountains and the Sea, Collated and. Translated], Shanghaï: Shanghai guji chubanshe, 1985.

Works and articles

*Anisensel, Aliénor, *Le sens d'une tradition élitiste dans le Viêt-Nam contemporain: pratiques, apprentissages et esthétiques du chant "Ca trù"*, doctoral thesis, Université Paris Ouest Nanterre – La Défense, 2012.

Bách khoa thư bằng tranh [Pictorial Encyclopaedia], Hà Nội: Viện từ điển Bách khoa, Ủy ban khoa học xã hội, 1985.

*Barrau, Jacques, "L'ethnobotanique au carrefour des sciences naturelles et des sciences humaines", *Bulletin de la Société Botanique de France*, 118 (1971), pp. 237–48.

Bibliography 233

*Cabaton, Antoine, *L'Indochine*, Paris: Renouard, H. Laurens, 1932.

*Cauchetier, Raymond, *Saigon*, Paris: Albin Michel, 1955.

*Coyaud, Maurice, *Cris des rues au Việt Nam* (Reprint of "Les marchands ambulants et les cris de la rue à Hanoï", *Revue Indochinoise*. s.l.n.d.), Paris: P.A.F. (Pour l'Analyse du Folklore), 1980.

*Crévost, Charles et Lemarié, Charles, *Catalogue des produits de l'Indochine*, t.I Produits alimentaires et Plantes fourragères, Gouvernement Général de l'Indochine, Hanoï: Imprimerie d'Extrême-Orient, 1917.

*Crouzet, Yves, *Travailler le bambou*, Paris: Actes Sud, 2005.

*Đào Duy Anh, "Les grandes familles de l'Annam, S.E. Trần Tiễn Thành", *Bulletin des Amis du Vieux Hué*, xxxiᵉ année, n° 2, avril-juin, 1944, pp. 91–160.

*Đinh Trọng Hiếu, "Les galets aménagés du Hoabinhien", dans Bersani, Jacques (ed.), *Le grand atlas de l'archéologie*, Paris: Encyclopaedia universalis France, 1985, pp. 288–9.

*Đinh Trọng Hiếu, "Une page commentée du *Lĩnh Nam Chích Quái* – Contes Extraordinaires du Lĩnh Nam (xvᵉ s.), sur les mœurs et coutumes des Vietnamiens primitifs", *Cahiers d'Études Vietnamiennes*, N° spécial, 7–8, Paris: 1985–1986, pp. 6–25.

*Đinh Trọng Hiếu, "Dĩ khương căn vi diêm (Lấy rễ gừng làm muối): Tương quan giữa tư liệu thư tịch và tư liệu thực địa" [Using ginger roots to make salt, text and field interactions], *Văn Lang*, Westminster, U.S.A., N° 3, 1992, pp. 5–37.

*Đinh Trọng Hiếu, "L'étude du Hoabinhien, une pluridisciplinarité effective", dans Cyril Dumas, Bertrand Roussel, Pierre-Jean Texier (ed.), *Langage de pierre, La restitution du geste en archéologie préhistorique*, colloque européen, Les Baux de Provence: Musée des Baux de Provence, 2009, pp. 24–31.

*Đinh Trọng Hiếu & Poisson, Emmanuel (dir.), *Hà Nội en couleurs, 1914–1917: Autochromes des archives de la planète*, Paris: Riveneuve, 2014.

*Dournes, Jacques, *Bois-Bambou, Aspect végétal de l'Univers Joraï*, Paris: Éditions du C.N.R.S., 1969.

*Dournes, Jacques, *La culture Jörai, Catalogues du Musée de l'Homme*, Paris: MNHN, addition to vol. XII, 2, Objets et Mondes, 1972.

*Dumoutier, Gustave, *Essais sur les Tonkinois*, Hanoi-Haiphong: Imprimerie d'Extrême-Orient, 1908.

*Durand, Maurice, *Imagerie populaire vietnamienne*, Paris: École française d'Extrême-Orient, 1960, reedition, 2011.

*Dutreuil de Rhins, Jules-Léon, *Le Royaume d'Annam et les Annamites, journal de voyage de J.-L. Dutreuil de Rhins*, Paris: E. Plon, 1889.

*Fanchette, Sylvie, Stedmann, Nicholas, *À la découverte des villages de métier au Việt Nam; dix itinéraires autour de Hanoi*, Marseille: IRD éd., 2009.

*Fradin, Marcel, *Perspective conique: tracé des ombres*, Paris: Dessain et Tolra, 1980.

*Gourou, Pierre, *Les paysans du delta tonkinois: Étude de géographie humaine*, Paris: Les Éditions d'Art et d'Histoire, 1936.

*Guilleminet, Paul, "Une industrie annamite: les norias du Quảng Ngãi", *Bulletin des Amis du Vieux Hué*, avril-juin 1926, 13ᵉ année, n° 2, pp. 97–232.

*Hockney, David, *Savoirs secrets. Les techniques perdues des maîtres anciens*, nlle éd. augmentée, Paris: Seuil, 2006.

*Hocquard, Édouard, *Une campagne au Tonkin*, Paris: Hachette, 1892. See also in Gallica. Available: https://gallica.bnf.fr/ark:/12148/bpt6k6336764z.r=Une%20campagne%20au%20Tonkin?rk=21459;2 [Accessed: 16/03/2020].

*Lajoux, Jean-Dominique, *Le tambour du déluge – villages des montagnes d'Indochine* (textes et photographies), Paris: Éditions du Seuil, 1977.

234 *Bibliography*

Monographie dessinée de l'Indochine. Publications by École d'art de Giadinh, Paris: Librairie orientaliste Paul Geuthner, 1935, Cochinchine, 6 vol., 240 pl., preface by Louis Malleret, pp. 1–11. Tonkin, 4 vol., 160 pl. Annam, 1 vol., 40 pl. Cambodge, Laos, 2 vol., 80 pl.

*Musée de la Monnaie de Paris, *Les collections monétaires VII, Monnaies d'Extrême Orient*, Paris: Administration des Monnaies et Médailles, 2 vol., 1986.

*National Bureau of Measurement, China History Museum and Palace Museum, *Zhongguo gudai duliangheng tuji* 中国古代度量衡图集 [A Collection of Illustrations of Ancient Chinese Weights and Measures], Pékin: Wenwu chubanshe, 1984.

*Nguyễn Huệ Chi, *Thơ văn Lý Trần* [Lý Trần period poems], Hà Nội: nhà xuất bản Khoa học xã hội, 1989, vol. 3.

*Nguyễn Văn Ngọc, *Tục ngữ phong dao* [Proverbs and folk songs], Hà Nội: Minh Đức xuất bản, 1957, 2 vol.

*Oger, Henri, *Technique du peuple annamite* [Mechanics and Crafts of the People of Annam], collection of wood engravings made by north-vietnamese craftsmen Nguyễn Văn Đang, Nguyễn Văn Giai, Phạm Văn Tiêu and Phạm Trọng Hải, Paris: Geuthner, 1909; reedition and preface by Olivier Tessier and Philippe Le Failler Hanoi: École Française d'Extrême-Orient, 2009, 3 vol. See also *Library of Congress*. Available: www.loc.gov/item/2021666950/

*Oprins, Jan et Van Trier, Harry, *Bambous*, Paris: Actes Sud, 2005.

*Poisson, Emmanuel, "Détruire ou consolider les digues du delta du fleuve Rouge. Un débat au sein de la haute bureaucratie vietnamienne au xixe siècle", *Aséanie* 23 (2009), pp. 77–96.

*Poisson, Emmanuel, "La confrontation textes-terrains dans la construction des savoirs par Lê Quý Đôn, lettré vietnamien du xviiie siècle", in Liliane Hilaire-Pérez, Valérie Nègre, Delphine Spicq, Koen Vermeir (eds.), *Le livre technique avant le xxe siècle à l'échelle du monde*, Paris: CNRS éditions, 2017, pp. 59–70.

*Portère, Roland, *Les sels alimentaires – cendres d'origine végétale, sels de cendres comme succédanés de chlorure de sodium alimentaire et catalogue des plantes salifères en Afrique intertropicale et à Madagascar*, Dakar: Direction Générale de la Santé publique, Gouvernement Général de l'Afrique Occidentale Française, 1950.

*Sarraut, Albert, *Indochine*, documents commentés par Charles Robequain, Paris: Firmin Didot, 1930.

*Stein, Rolf, *Le monde en petit: jardins en miniature et habitations dans la pensée religieuse d'Extrême-Orient*, Paris, Flammarion, 1987.

*Thierry, François, *Catalogue des monnaies vietnamiennes*, Paris: BnF, 1988.

*Thierry, François, *Catalogue des monnaies vietnamiennes, Supplément*, Paris: BnF, 2002.

*Weber, Nicolas, *Contribution à l'histoire des communautés cam en Asie du Sud-Est (Cambodge, Vietnam, Siam, Malaisie): intégration politique, militaire et économique*, doctoral thesis, Paris: Inalco, 2005, 2 vol.

Discography

*Kersalé, Patrick, *Musiques aux pays des bambous*, DVD documentary. 2009, Ed. Lugdivine. Ethnys. 7352.

*Mission Frantz Laforest, *Musique Proto Indochinoise*, collected from the Highland Moïs. BAM (La Boîte à Musique), LD 326.- France. 33 LP disk 1/3.1955.

Musique Mnong Gar du Vietnam, Anthologie de musique Proto-Indochinoise, vol. 1. Enregistrements, photographies et notices: Condominas, Georges, Collection du Musée de l'homme, Département d'ethnomusicologie. Disques OCORA. 33 tours.

Vietnam. Musique des Montagnards, 2 CD. Le chant du Monde, Collection du C.N.R.S. et du Musée de l'Homme. ACCT. CD 1: Vietnam du Centre, Jörai, Bahnar, Edê, Srê, Lac, Ma. 1997.67.57'. CD 2: Vietnam du Nord, Hani, Yao, Hmong, Nung, Pa-y, Thaï, Khmu, Muong, 1997.

Index

Bahnar 52, 218
bương 7, 39, 41, *41*

chặt 24, 26, 86, *86*
chẻ 22, 26, 64, 149, *149*
Chỉ nam ngọc âm giải nghĩa. 指南玉音解
    義 33n8, 196n18
cối xay *185*, *186*, 203, *223*
cót *70*, 71, 168, 171, *171*, 173, 205

Dai Kaizhi 戴凱之 2n1, 24, 34, 58n2, 77,
    79n65
đan 22, *126*, *127*, *128*, *155*, *157*
đẵn 26, 63
đàn tập tình 53, 58n13
đàn t'rưng 52, 58n10, 218, *219*
Đào Xá *12*, 35, *36*, *48*, *49*, 69, *70*, *191*,
    222, 223
đing pâng 52, *53*
đòn gánh 22, 23, 207
Dumoutier, Gustave (1850–1904) 81, 123,
    126, 159

gầu *192*, 193, *193*, 194, *194*, *195*,
    196n18
giần 177, 180, *180*, 182, 183, *183*
giậu 16, 22, *134*
Gióng 13, 14, *14*

Hocquard, Charles-Edouard (1853–1911)
    37, 81, 96, 116, 220

Ji Han 稽含 2n1, 52

Kontum 52, 218

lạt cật 27, *29*, *30*, 175
lạt ruột *29*, 31, *32*, 175

Lê Quý Đôn 黎貴惇 (1726–1784) 2, 34,
    35, 58n2, 59, 60, 71, 77, 78, 79n68,
    139, 223
liếp 16, 22, *28*, *171*
Loureiro, João de (?-1791) 63, 223

măng 18, *18*, 23, 24, 61, 62, 65, 83, *84*, 86

Nguyễn Trãi 阮廌 (1380–1442) 15, 59, 63, 64
nia 22, 171, 177, 178, *178*, 183, 184
nơm (carafe-shaped trap) 18, 19, 190, *191*,
    193, *227*, *228*
nôm (vietnamese vernacular writting) 2, 17,
    18, 19, 33n5, 63, 65n4, 82, *115*
nong 22, 171, 177, 178, *178*, 180, 184
nứa 22, 35, 37, 50, 51, 52, 53, *120*, 133, *178*, 223

Oger, Henri (1885–?) 2, 33n8, 81, 107n4,
    128, 197, 206

palanquin 69, *70*, 78n19
phên 22, *28*, 64, 161, *162*, 168, 187

quạt 22, *157*, 158, *158*, 171, *172*, 177, 196n3

rá 22, 163, *175*, 176
raft (bè) 37, 38, *38*, *39*, 77, 88, *91*, 93, *93*
Rhodes, Alexandre de (1593–1660) *20*, 21,
    22, 26, 33n10, 63
rổ 22, *155*, 163, 164, 176, *176*

sàng 22, 177, 180, *181*, 182, *182*, 184
sọt 22, 76, *175*
staff of old age 9, *12*, 23, 48, *48*
swing (đu) *44*, *94–96*, 95

tam tinh 8, 9, 23, *48*, *49*, 114
tầm vông 7, 61, 77, 216

tang koa 53, 54, *55*, 58n14
thúng 22, 174, 184, 207
thuyền thúng 160, 165, 166, 167, *168*
tre 1, 7, *7, 14, 18*, 19, 21, 22, 23, 24, 25,
    25, 26, 50, 61, 62, 63, 64, 69,
    70, 85, 86, 92, 101, 105, 113,
    115, 122, 134, 136, 154, *157*,
    160, 221
trúc 7, 9, 16, 22, 23, 34, 47, 48, 49, 60, 63,
    64, 65, 68, 69, 74, 75, 77, 79n39,

90, 112, 114, 116, 120, *121, 123,*
    128, *137*, 175

vót 27, 50, 154, 161
Vương Hồng Sển (1902–1996) 22, 23, 46,
    64, 83, 210

Wang Zhen 王禎 (1271–1368) 178, 196n14,
    196n16
waterwheel 40, *42–43*, 58n6

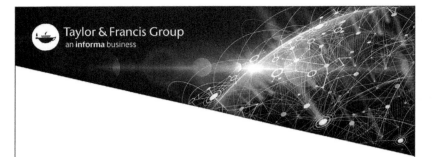

9781032395722